Busy Ant Maths

Progress Guide 3

Series Editor: Peter Clarke

Authors: Elizabeth Jurgensen, Jeanette Mumford, Sandra Roberts

William Collins' dream of knowledge for all began with the publication of his first book in 1819. A self-educated mill worker, he not only enriched millions of lives, but also founded a flourishing publishing house. Today, staying true to this spirit, Collins books are packed with inspiration, innovation and practical expertise. They place you at the centre of a world of possibility and give you exactly what you need to explore it.

Collins. Freedom to teach.

Published by Collins
An imprint of HarperCollins*Publishers*
77–85 Fulham Palace Road
Hammersmith
London
W6 8JB

> Browse the complete Collins catalogue at
> **www.collins.co.uk**

10 9 8 7 6 5 4 3

ISBN 978-0-00-756243-5

British Library Cataloguing in Publication Data
A Catalogue record for this publication is available from the British Library

Publishing Manager: Fiona McGlade
Managing Editor: Sarah Thomas
Project editors: Hamish Baxter and Leah Willey
Production: Rachel Weaver
Editors: Catherine Dakin, Donna Cole and Jean Rustean
Cover design and artwork: Amparo Barrera
Internal design concept: Amparo Barrera
Designed: Neil Adams, Grasshopper Design Company
Illustrations: Louise Forshaw, Eva Sassin, Gwyneth Williamson and Steven Woods

Printed and bound by Martins the Printers Ltd, Berwick-upon-Tweed

Contents

Unit 3

Week 1: **Number – Addition and subtraction**
Lesson 1, Support: Adding 1s
Lesson 2, Extension: Missing numbers (1)
Lesson 3, Support: Counting on in 100s
Lesson 4, Extension: Shopping problems

Week 2: **Number – Addition and subtraction**
Lesson 1, Support: Subtracting 1s
Lesson 2, Extension: Missing numbers (2)
Lesson 3, Support: Counting back in 100s
Lesson 4, Extension: Swimming problems

Week 3: **Geometry – Properties of shape**
Lesson 2, Extension: More robot patterns
Lesson 3, Support: Turning the hands
Lesson 3, Extension: Taking turns
Lesson 4, Support: All sorts of fans

Unit 4

Week 1: **Number – Multiplication and division, including Number and place value**
Lesson 2, Support: 4 multiplication table
Lesson 3, Support: Doubling to find the 4 multiplication table
Lesson 3, Extension: Speedy multiplication tables
Lesson 4, Extension: Multiplication and division of 4

Week 2: **Number – Multiplication and division, including Number and place value**
Lesson 2, Support: 8 multiplication table
Lesson 3, Support: Doubling to find the 8 multiplication table
Lesson 3, Extension: Doubling to find the 4 and 8 multiplication tables
Lesson 4, Extension: All things 8: solving word problems

Week 3: **Measurement (time)**
Lesson 1, Support: Time to the minute
Lesson 2, Extension: Olympics time line
Lesson 3, Support: Roman dials and station clocks
Lesson 3, Extension: Station times

Unit 5

Week 1: **Number – Number and place value**
Lesson 1, Support: Making 3-digit numbers
Lesson 1, Extension: Larger number wins
Lesson 3, Extension: How much money?
Lesson 4, Support: Find your way

Week 2: **Number – Addition and subtraction, including Measurement (money)**
Lesson 1, Support: Amounts of money
Lesson 2, Extension: How much change?
Lesson 3, Support: Calculating change
Lesson 4, Extension: Furniture shop

Week 3: **Geometry – Properties of shape**
Lesson 2, Support: New shapes from old
Lesson 2, Extension: Triangles in a row
Lesson 3, Support: Exploring shapes
Lesson 3, Extension: Exploring shapes

Unit 6

Week 1: **Number – Multiplication and division, including Number and place value**
Lesson 1, Extension: Counting in steps of 2, 4 and 8
Lesson 3, Support: Halving to find the division facts (1)
Lesson 3, Support: Halving to find the division facts (2)
Lesson 4, Extension: Solving word problems

Week 2: **Number – Fractions**
Lesson 1, Support: Finding quarters
Lesson 2, Extension: Non-unit fractions
Lesson 3, Extension: Fraction diagrams
Lesson 4, Support: Shading number lines

Week 3: **Measurement (length)**
Lesson 2, Support: Millimetres of bracelets
Lesson 2, Extension: Spirals in millimetres
Lesson 3, Support: Comparing lengths
Lesson 3, Extension: Skateboard jumps

Unit 7

Week 1: **Number – Addition and subtraction**
  Lesson 1, Support: Adding 1s and 10s
  Lesson 2, Extension: Adding instructions
  Lesson 3, Extension: Addition puzzle
  Lesson 4, Support: Add numbers mentally

Week 2: **Number – Addition and subtraction, including Measurement (money)**
  Lesson 1, Support: Subtracting 1s and 10s
  Lesson 2, Extension: Subtracting instructions
  Lesson 3, Support: Subtracting 10s and 100s
  Lesson 4, Extension: Sports problems

Week 3: **Statistics**
  Lesson 1, Support: Fruit and vegetable charts
  Lesson 2, Support: Counters pictogram
  Lesson 2, Extension: Dice pictograms
  Lesson 3, Extension: Capacity bar chart

Unit 8

Week 1: **Number – Multiplication and division, including Number and place value**
  Lesson 2, Support: Revising multiplication facts
  Lesson 2, Extension: Revising multiplication facts
  Lesson 3, Support: Revising division facts
  Lesson 4, Extension: Solving problems

Week 2: **Number – Fractions**
  Lesson 1, Extension: Pizza problem
  Lesson 2, Support: Subtracting snakes
  Lesson 2, Extension: Subtracting beyond 1 whole
  Lesson 4, Support: Building fractions

Week 3: **Measurement (perimeter)**
  Lesson 2, Support: Perimeters of rectangles
  Lesson 2, Extension: Predicting perimeters
  Lesson 3, Support: Perimeter patterns
  Lesson 4, Extension: Hexagonal hunt

Unit 9

Week 1: **Number – Number and place value**
Lesson 1, Extension: Digit sum tickets
Lesson 2, Support: On the number line
Lesson 3, Extension: Find my number
Lesson 4, Support: Circle the numbers

Week 2: **Number – Addition and subtraction**
Lesson 1, Support: Mental addition and subtraction
Lesson 2, Extension: Challenge your partner (1)
Lesson 3, Extension: Challenge your partner (2)
Lesson 4, Support: Word problems

Week 3: **Geometry – Properties of shape**
Lesson 1, Extension: Drawing spirals
Lesson 2, Support: Pairs of lines
Lesson 2, Extension: Lines on a 9-dot grid
Lesson 3, Support: Shape shopping list

Unit 10

Week 1: **Number – Multiplication and division**
Lesson 1, Support: Multiplication using partitioning
Lesson 2, Support: Multiplication using partitioning and the grid method
Lesson 3, Extension: Multiplication: Introducing the expanded written method
Lesson 4, Extension: Solving problems

Week 2: **Number – Fractions**
Lesson 1, Support: Finding fractions
Lesson 2, Extension: Pound fractions
Lesson 3, Extension: Equivalent patterns
Lesson 4, Support: Tenths on number lines

Week 3: **Measurement (volume and capacity)**
Lesson 1, Support: Measuring cylinders
Lesson 1, Extension: Fractions full or empty
Lesson 2, Support: Go-kart millilitres
Lesson 3, Extension: Measuring in millilitres

Unit 11

Week 1: **Number – Addition and subtraction, including Measurement (money)**
Lesson 1, Support: Estimating
Lesson 2, Extension: Make 900
Lesson 4, Support: School shopping
Lesson 4, Extension: Kitting out Thomas

Week 2: **Number – Addition and subtraction**
Lesson 1, Support: Break it down
Lesson 2, Extension: Make 600
Lesson 3, Extension: Clever jumping
Lesson 4, Support: Jumping backwards

Week 3: **Measurement (time)**
Lesson 1, Support: Digital and wall clocks
Lesson 3, Support: Days of the month
Lesson 3, Extension: Calendar counting
Lesson 4, Extension: Measuring time

Unit 12

Week 1: **Number – Multiplication and division**
Lesson 1, Support: Multiplication using the expanded written method
Lesson 2, Support: Multiplication: Introducing the formal written method
Lesson 3, Extension: Multiplication: Introducing the formal written method
Lesson 4, Extension: Solving problems

Week 2: **Number – Multiplication and division**
Lesson 1, Support: Division using partitioning
Lesson 3, Support: Division using the formal written method
Lesson 3, Extension: Division using the formal written method
Lesson 4, Extension: Solving word problems

Week 3: **Statistics**
Lesson 2, Support: Savings bar chart
Lesson 2, Extension: Racing game bar chart
Lesson 3, Support: Dice spots pictogram
Lesson 4, Extension: Bags of fruit bar chart

Name: _____ Date: _____

0s and 1s

Understand the 10s and 1s in 2-digit numbers

Look at the 1–50 square and choose a number.

Make that number using Base 10.
Put the 10s in the 10s circle and
the 1s in the 1s circle.

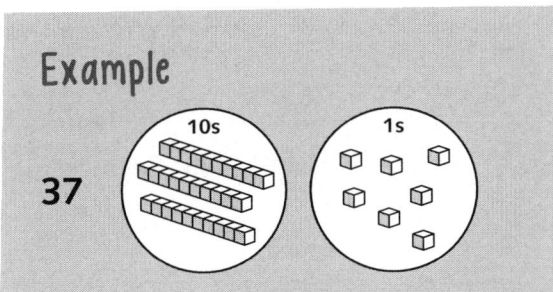

1	2	3	4	5	6	7	8	9	10
11	12	13	14	15	16	17	18	19	20
21	22	23	24	25	26	27	28	29	30
31	32	33	34	35	36	37	38	39	40
41	42	43	44	45	46	47	48	49	50

10s   **1s**

Then write your number as a calculation.

Repeat until you have nine calculations.

Example $30 + 7 = 37$

1 ☐ + ☐ = ☐   2 ☐ + ☐ = ☐   3 ☐ + ☐ = ☐

4 ☐ + ☐ = ☐   5 ☐ + ☐ = ☐   6 ☐ + ☐ = ☐

7 ☐ + ☐ = ☐   8 ☐ + ☐ = ☐   9 ☐ + ☐ = ☐

Name: _____ Date: _____

What's my number?

Recognise the place value of each digit in a 2-digit number

1 I am thinking of a 2-digit number. The 10s digit is higher than 7 and the 1s digit is even. What could my number be? Write as many possible answers as you can.

2 I am thinking of a 2-digit number. The 10s digit is between 3 and 7 and the 1s digit is odd. What could my number be? Write as many possible answers as you can.

3 Make up a similar problem for your friend to work out. They can write their answers in the thought bubbles below.

_____

_____

_____

Name: _____ Date: _____

ounting to 200

Understand numbers beyond 100

1 Complete the number square.

101									
								119	
			124						
	152								
							168		
				175					
									200

2 • Cut out the number square along the thick lines to make 17 pieces.

• Mix up all the pieces.

• Put the number square back together. How quickly can you do it?

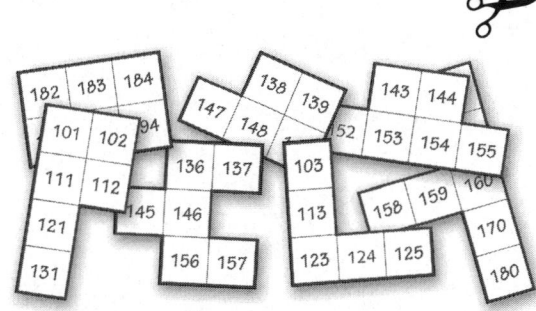

Name: _____ Date: _____

Finding all the 3-digit numbers

Solve number problems

1 Make as many 3-digit numbers as you can using these 4 numbers and write them below.

Check that all your numbers are different!

2 Now write your numbers in a systematic way.

Explain your system.

_____

_____

Name: _____ Date: _____

Adding on a number line

Add two 2-digit numbers mentally

Example

23 + 14 = 37

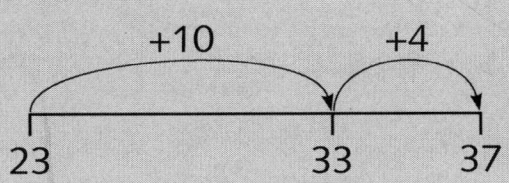

1 Complete these calculations.

a 15 + 14 = ☐

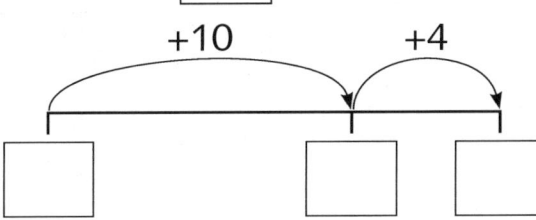

b 17 + 12 = ☐

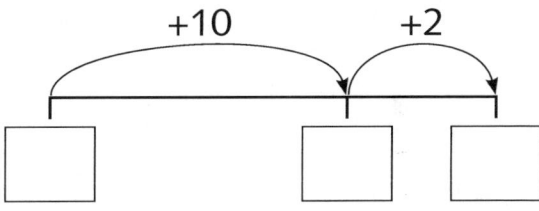

c 24 + 13 = ☐

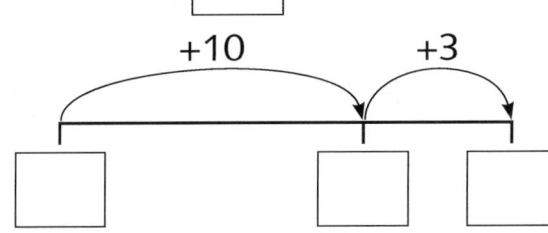

d 26 + 14 = ☐

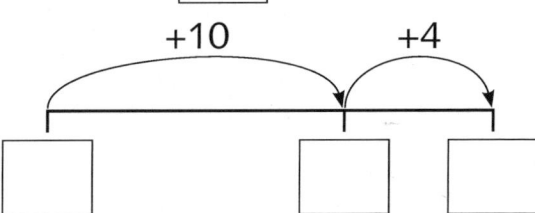

2 Now draw the jumps on the number lines yourself.

a 25 + 13 = ☐

b 22 + 16 = ☐

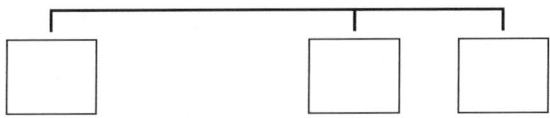

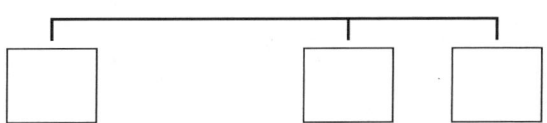

c 27 + 21 = ☐

d 26 + 22 = ☐

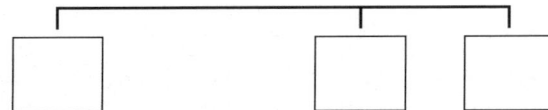

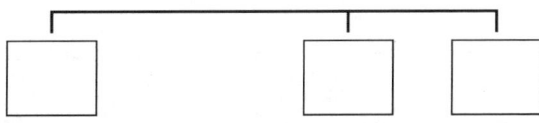

Name: _____ Date: _____

Is and 10s race

Add mentally 1s and 10s to a 3-digit number

You will need:
• 1–6 dice

Jump to the target

Play this game with a partner.

This could be 3 or 30.

• Take turns to:
  – roll the dice
  – decide whether to use your number as 1s or 10s
  – jump that many along the number line
    from the starting number.

• The winner is the first player to reach the target number.

• Play three times.

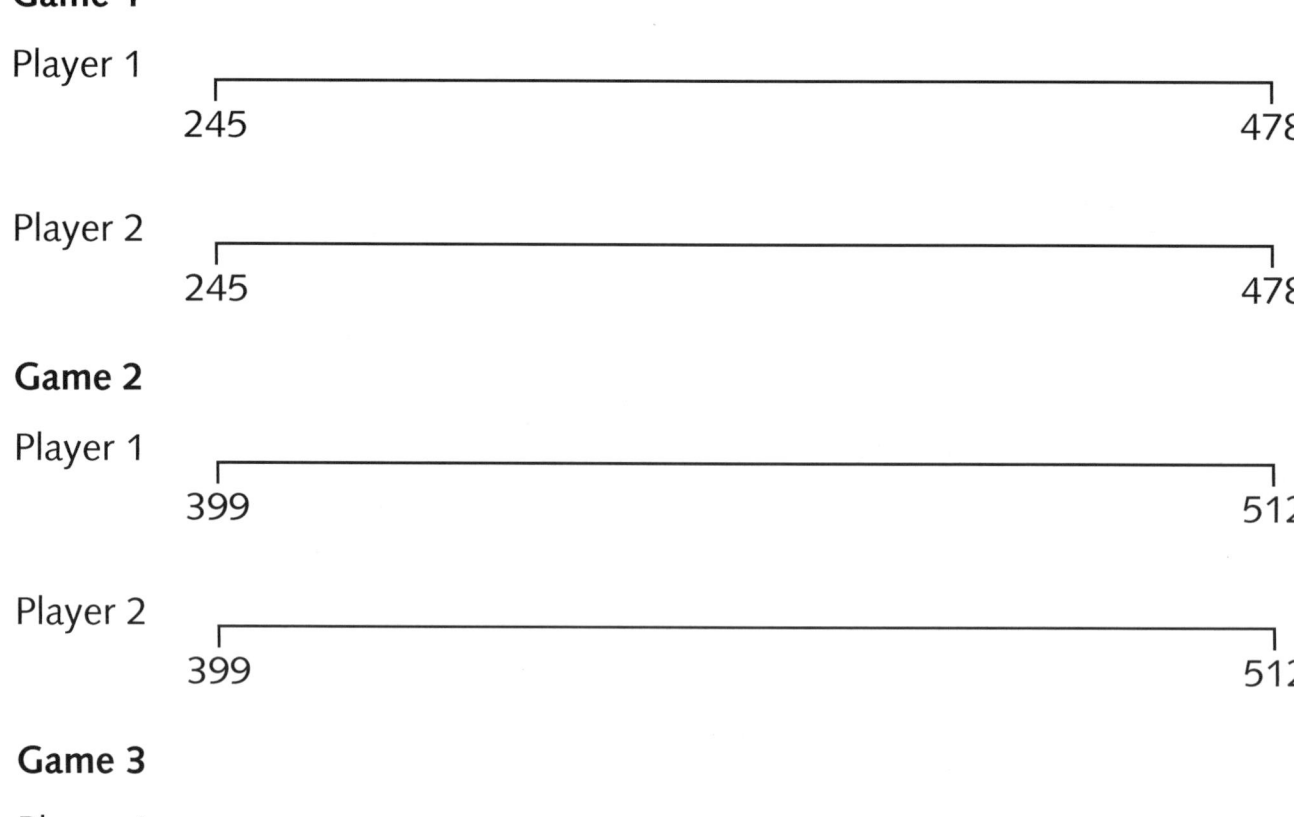

Game 1

Player 1

245   478

Player 2

245   478

Game 2

Player 1

399   512

Player 2

399   512

Game 3

Player 1

384   603

Player 2

384   603

Name: _____ Date: _____

Subtracting 10s

Subtract mentally a 2-digit number and 10s

1 Choose a number in the 90s on the number square and colour it in.

1	2	3	4	5	6	7	8	9	10
11	12	13	14	15	16	17	18	19	20
21	22	23	24	25	26	27	28	29	30
31	32	33	34	35	36	37	38	39	40
41	42	43	44	45	46	47	48	49	50
51	52	53	54	55	56	57	58	59	60
61	62	63	64	65	66	67	68	69	70
71	72	73	74	75	76	77	78	79	80
81	82	83	84	85	86	87	88	89	90
91	92	93	94	95	96	97	98	99	100

- Subtract 10 and colour in the answer.

- Keep going backwards to the top row of the square.

- Write the numbers in the boxes below. Do you see the pattern?

2 Choose a different number in the 90s on the number square.

- Write your starting number in the first box then write the numbers you get when subtracting 10 here – no colouring this time!

3 a $16 - 10 =$ ☐   **b** $24 - 10 =$ ☐   **c** $27 - 10 =$ ☐

d $31 - 10 =$ ☐   **e** $38 - 10 =$ ☐   **f** $47 - 10 =$ ☐

4 a $28 - 20 =$ ☐   **b** $42 - 20 =$ ☐   **c** $29 - 20 =$ ☐

d $53 - 20 =$ ☐   **e** $37 - 20 =$ ☐   **f** $66 - 20 =$ ☐

Name: _____ Date: _____

What's the calculation?

Subtract two 2-digit numbers mentally

Write six different calculations for each question.

1 a ☐ − ☐ = 27   **b** ☐ − ☐ = 27

c ☐ − ☐ = 27   **d** ☐ − ☐ = 27

e ☐ − ☐ = 27   **f** ☐ − ☐ = 27

2 a ☐ − ☐ = 41   **b** ☐ − ☐ = 41

c ☐ − ☐ = 41   **d** ☐ − ☐ = 41

e ☐ − ☐ = 41   **f** ☐ − ☐ = 41

3 a 39 = ☐ − ☐   **b** 39 = ☐ − ☐

c 39 = ☐ − ☐   **d** 39 = ☐ − ☐

e 39 = ☐ − ☐   **f** 39 = ☐ − ☐

4 a 53 = ☐ − ☐   **b** 53 = ☐ − ☐

c 53 = ☐ − ☐   **d** 53 = ☐ − ☐

e 53 = ☐ − ☐   **f** 53 = ☐ − ☐

5 a 61 = ☐ − ☐   **b** 61 = ☐ − ☐

c 61 = ☐ − ☐   **d** 61 = ☐ − ☐

e 61 = ☐ − ☐   **f** 61 = ☐ − ☐

Name: _____ Date: _____

Building 3-D shapes

Recognise and name different prisms

1 Jonny used flat shapes to build these 3-D models. Colour the shapes with these end faces as follows:

You will need:
• green, yellow, red and blue pencils

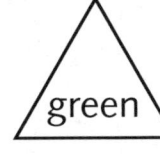 green yellow red blue

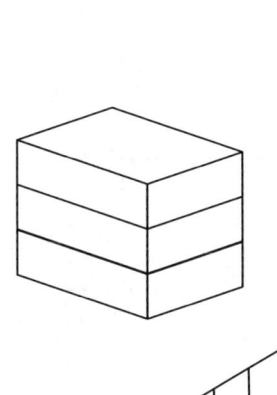
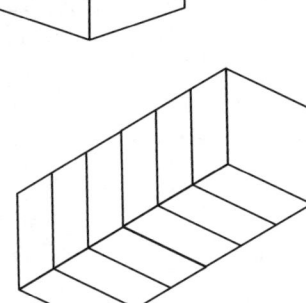

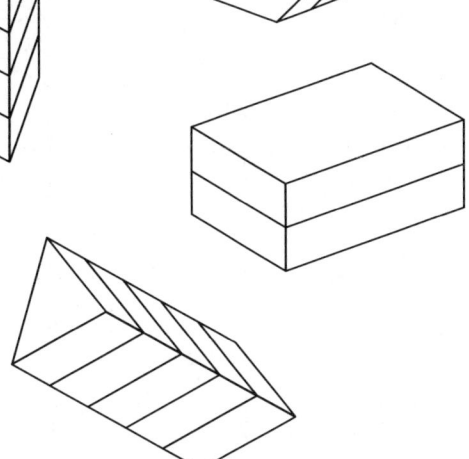
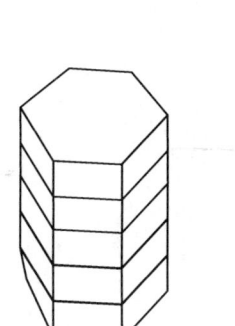

2 Match the colour to the name of the shape with an arrow.

green

blue

yellow

red

square prisms

triangular prisms

rectangular prisms

hexagonal prisms

Name: _____ Date: _____

3-D spreadsheet

Make models of 3-D shapes using 2-D shapes

1 How many of each 2-D shape do you need to make a model of each 3-D shape?

		2-D face				
		△	☐	▭	⬠	⬡
3-D shape	a					
	b					
	c					
	d					
	e					
	f					

2 a Make a model of a cylinder.

You will need:
- sheet of card
- ruler
- plastic circle
- scissors
- sticky tape

b On the back of this sheet, describe how you made your model of a cylinder.

Name: _____ Date: _____

Describing sweet shapes

Describe 3-D shapes

Lena sorts the sweets then puts them into packets.
Decide which packet each sweet will go into.
Write the letter on the packet.

A sweet can go into more than one packet.

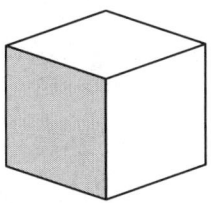

A cube

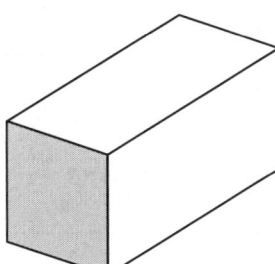

B cuboid with
square end face

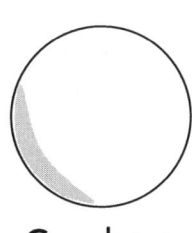

C sphere

D triangular prism

E hemisphere

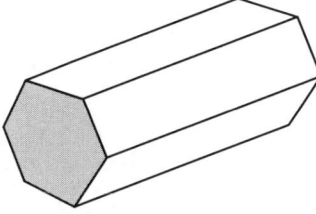

F hexagonal prism

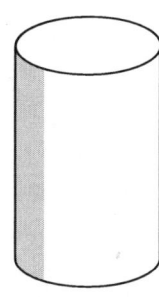

H cylinder

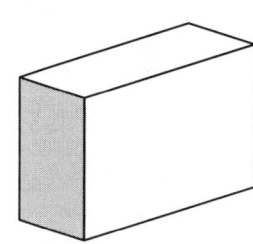

I cuboid

G cone

**Peppermint
prisms**

**Fruity
five faces**

**Raspberry
rectangles**

**Caramel
curves**

Name: _____ Date: _____

Properties of pyramids

Use properties of 3-D shapes to describe pyramids

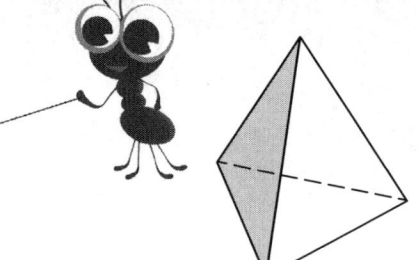

1 Complete the table.

Pyramid base	Number of sides of base	Number of faces of pyramid
Triangle	3	4
Square		
Pentagon		
Hexagon		
Heptagon		
Octagon		

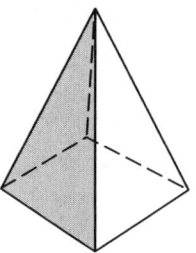

2 Predict the number of faces for a pyramid with a base of:

a 10 sides ☐   **b** 12 sides ☐

3 Complete the table.

Pyramid base	Number of sides of base	Number of edges of pyramid
Triangle	3	6
Square		
Pentagon		
Hexagon		
Heptagon		
Octagon		

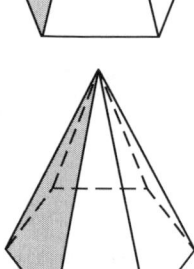

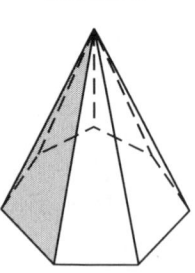

4 Predict the number of edges for a pyramid with a base of:

a 10 sides ☐   **b** 12 sides ☐

5 Is there a relationship between the number of sides of the base of a pyramid and the number of its vertices? Use the other side of this sheet to draw a table similar to those in Questions 1 and 3 for the number of vertices of a pyramid. Predict the number of vertices for pyramids with bases of 10 and 12 sides.

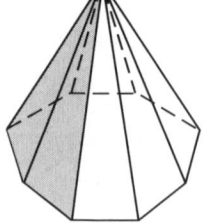

Name: _____ Date: _____

s, 5s and 10s

Recall the multiplication and division facts for the 2, 5 and 10 multiplication tables

1 Fill in the answers to the key facts for the × 2, × 5 and × 10 multiplication tables.

a 1 × 2 = ☐   e 1 × 5 = ☐   i 1 × 10 = ☐

b 2 × 2 = ☐   f 2 × 5 = ☐   j 2 × 10 = ☐

c 5 × 2 = ☐   g 5 × 5 = ☐   k 5 × 10 = ☐

d 10 × 2 = ☐   h 10 × 5 = ☐   l 10 × 10 = ☐

2 Use the key facts above to work out the answers to these facts. Write in the thought bubble which key fact helped you.

a (10 × 2 = 20)   l
b   9 × 2 = 18   m   12 × 5 = ☐
c   6 × 2 = ☐   n   8 × 5 = ☐
d   11 × 2 = ☐   o   3 × 5 = ☐
e   8 × 2 = ☐   p   6 × 10 = ☐
f   3 × 2 = ☐   q   9 × 10 = ☐
g   12 × 2 = ☐   r   3 × 10 = ☐
h   7 × 2 = ☐   s   11 × 10 = ☐
i   6 × 5 = ☐   t   8 × 10 = ☐
j   4 × 5 = ☐   u   4 × 10 = ☐
k   9 × 5 = ☐   12 × 10 = ☐
                           7 × 5 = ☐

Name: _____ Date: _____

3 multiplication table

Recall the multiplication facts for the 3 multiplication table

Play this game with a partner.

What to do:

You will need:
• 20 counters

• Cover each number fact with a counter.

• Take turns to:
  – remove a counter
  – say the answer to the multiplication fact.

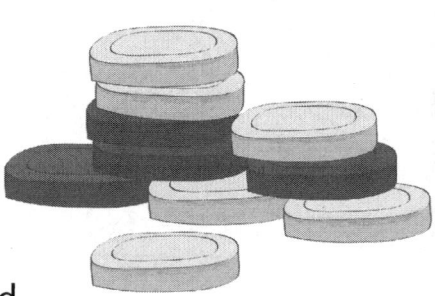

• If you are correct, keep the counter; if you are incorrect, place the counter back on the board.

• Continue until all the counters have been removed.

• The player with the most counters at the end is the winner.

3 × 6	3 × 5	7 × 3	11 × 3
5 × 3	3 × 2	3 × 4	3 × 5
10 × 3	1 × 3	3 × 9	12 × 3
9 × 3	6 × 3	3 × 3	3 × 10
8 × 3	3 × 7	4 × 3	3 × 8

Name: _____ Date: _____

What's my number?

Solve problems involving the 2, 3, 5 and 10 multiplication tables

1 Discover the numbers.

a Find two numbers that multiply to give 24, and where the two numbers also add up to 11.	**b** I'm thinking of a number. If I divide it by 2 then multiply it by 3, the answer is 21. What's the number?
c I'm thinking of a number. If I divide it by 3, then add 6, the answer is 16. What's the number?	**d** I think of a number, multiply it by 9 and then subtract 2. I'm left with 25. What's my number?
e Find the two numbers that multiply to give 40, and where the two numbers also add up to 13.	**f** I begin with a number, double it then times it by 3. From that number I take away 12. The answer is 12. What's my number?

2 Write your own 'What's my number?' problems involving the 3 multiplication table. Then give them to a friend to solve.

Name: _____ Date: _____

3 in a row

Recall the multiplication and division facts for the 2, 3, 5 and 10 multiplication tables

1 Circle the multiplication and division families for the 2, 3, 5 and 10 multiplication tables in the grid below. The numbers can go horizontally and vertically. There are 20 sets of numbers to find.

2 Write a multiplication fact or a division fact in the box below as you find each one.

60	24	7	2	14	10	20	5	4
5	30	45	9	5	24	3	8	16
12	6	25	3	4	12	18	2	9
13	5	32	30	8	2	16	90	42
17	16	10	8	80	46	31	9	29
3	5	15	11	43	10	25	3	18
36	7	3	21	27	5	5	3	6
12	23	14	31	3	50	5	95	3
3	2	6	12	9	100	10	10	67

Multiplication facts	Division facts
	$14 \div 2 = 7$

Name: _____ Date: _____

Finding halves

Divide objects into halves

You will need:
• 18 cubes or counters

1 One by one, count out the number of objects in Question **a**.
- Divide them in half by placing them on the tray above.
- Count how many are in each half.
- Fill in the answer below.
- Repeat for Questions **b–h**.

a 10 $\frac{1}{2}$ of 10 = ☐   **b** 6 $\frac{1}{2}$ of 6 = ☐

c 12 $\frac{1}{2}$ of 12 = ☐   **d** 8 $\frac{1}{2}$ of 8 = ☐

e 16 $\frac{1}{2}$ of 16 = ☐   **f** 4 $\frac{1}{2}$ of 4 = ☐

g 14 $\frac{1}{2}$ of 14 = ☐   **h** 18 $\frac{1}{2}$ of 18 = ☐

2 Explain what you did to find half.

_____

_____

_____

Name: _____ Date: _____

Quarter it

Solve a fraction problem

1 How many ways can you find to shade a quarter of the shape? ☐

Check that all your ways are different. Cross out any that are the same.

Name: _____ Date: _____

Practical fractions

Find fractions of amounts

1 Sort the counters into colours. Put one in each box below, keeping the same colours next to each other.

Write how many tenths of each colour you have.

$\frac{1}{10}$	$\frac{1}{10}$	$\frac{1}{10}$	$\frac{1}{10}$	$\frac{1}{10}$	$\frac{1}{10}$	$\frac{1}{10}$	$\frac{1}{10}$	$\frac{1}{10}$	$\frac{1}{10}$

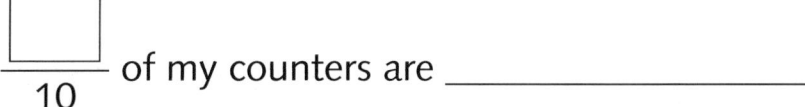 of my counters are _____

$\dfrac{\quad}{10}$ of my counters are _____

$\dfrac{\quad}{10}$ of my counters are _____

2 Now take 10 different counters, in four different colours, and do it again.

$\frac{1}{10}$	$\frac{1}{10}$	$\frac{1}{10}$	$\frac{1}{10}$	$\frac{1}{10}$	$\frac{1}{10}$	$\frac{1}{10}$	$\frac{1}{10}$	$\frac{1}{10}$	$\frac{1}{10}$

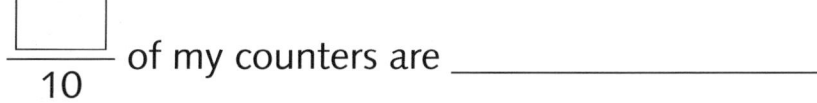 of my counters are _____

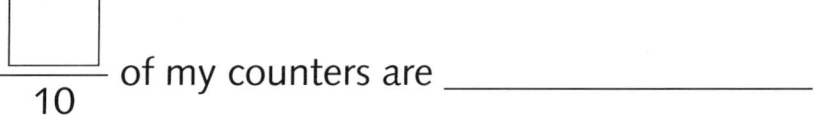 of my counters are _____

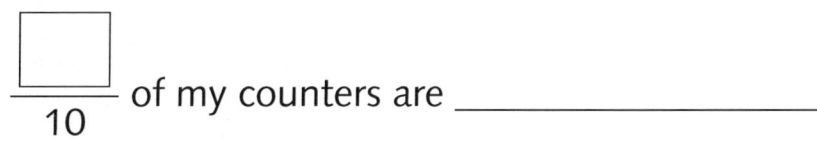 of my counters are _____

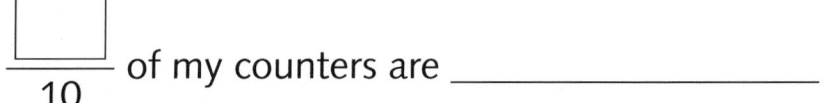 of my counters are _____

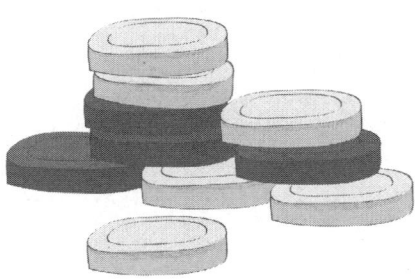

Name: _____ Date: _____

How many ways?

Add fractions with the same denominator

1 How many different fraction addition calculations can you find
that equal $\frac{10}{10}$?

Write them down here. You can add two or three fractions together.

> **Example** $\frac{3}{10} + \frac{5}{10} + \frac{2}{10} = \frac{10}{10}$

1 _____ 2 _____

3 _____ 4 _____

5 _____ 6 _____

7 _____ 8 _____

9 _____ 10 _____

11 _____ 12 _____

13 _____ 14 _____

15 _____ 16 _____

17 _____ 18 _____

19 _____ 20 _____

2 Choose one of your additions and explain how you know it is correct.

_____

_____

_____

Name: _____ Date: _____

On the scales

Read scales to the nearest division

1 Draw hands to show each mass.

a 2 kg

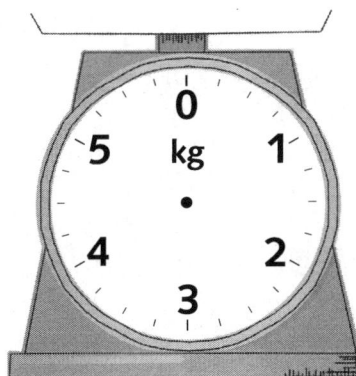

b $4\frac{1}{2}$ kg

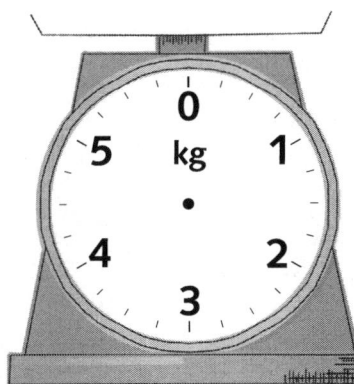

c $3\frac{1}{4}$ kg

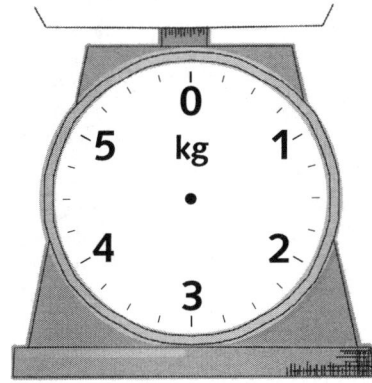

2 Write each mass on these scales in grams.

a

[ ] g

b

[ ] g

c

[ ] g

d

[ ] g

3 Write each mass in two ways.

a
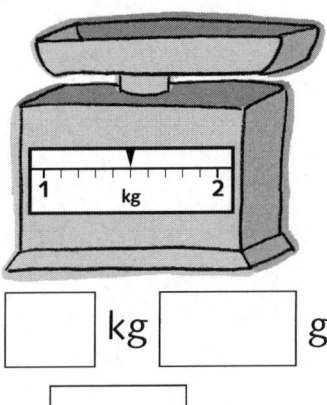

[ ] kg [ ] g

or [ ] g

b
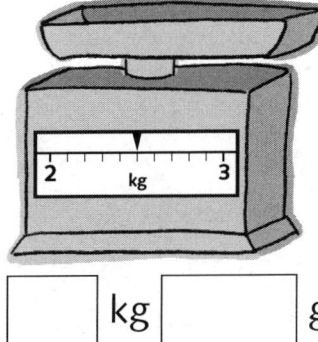

[ ] kg [ ] g

or [ ] g

c
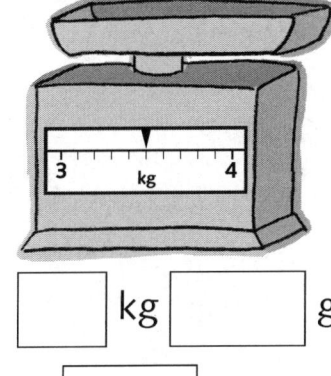

[ ] kg [ ] g

or [ ] g

Name: _____ Date: _____

Reading scales

Read scales marked in grams

1 Write each mass to the nearest 50 g. Then halve and double each mass.

a

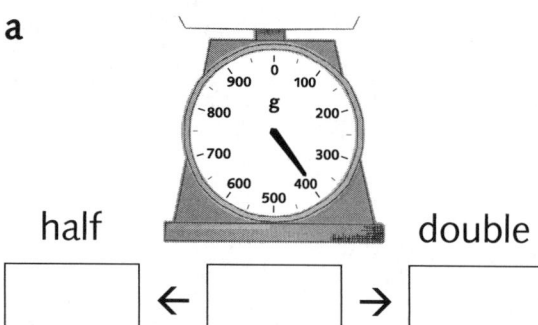

half [   ] ← [   ] → double [   ]

b

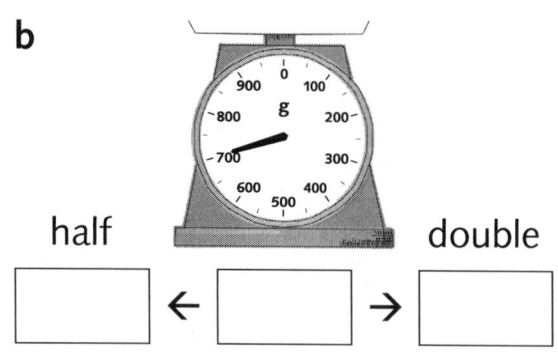

half [   ] ← [   ] → double [   ]

c

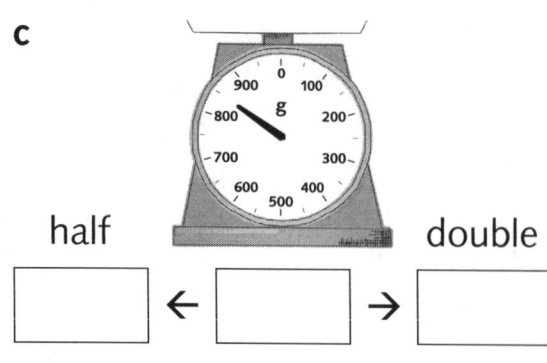

half [   ] ← [   ] → double [   ]

2 Use the clues to work out the mass. Draw the hand on the dial for the mass.

a

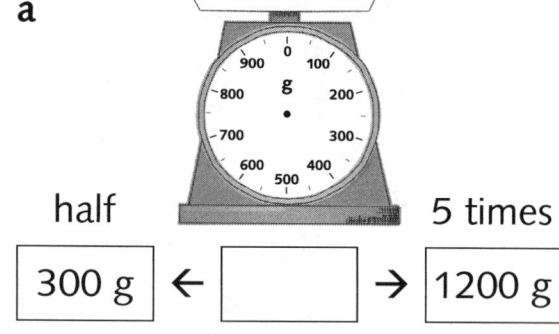

half [300 g] ← [   ] → 5 times [1200 g]

b

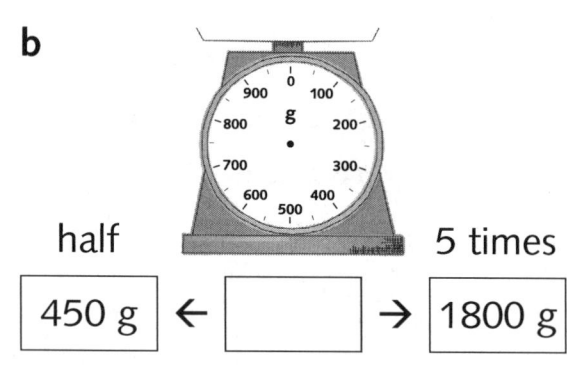

half [450 g] ← [   ] → 5 times [1800 g]

c

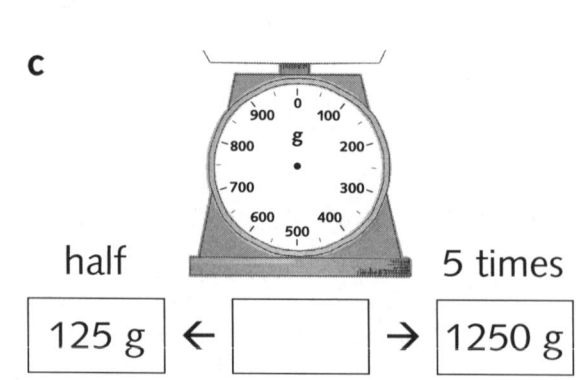

half [125 g] ← [   ] → 5 times [1250 g]

3 Three puppies together weigh 50 kg. The terrier and the spaniel puppies together weigh the same as the retriever puppy. The spaniel is 5 kg lighter than the terrier. What does each puppy weigh?

Terrier: [   ] kg   Spaniel: [   ] kg   Retriever: [   ] kg

Name: _____ Date: _____

More or less mass

Add and subtract mass

You will need:
- paper clip and pencil – for the spinner
- coin
- scissors

Play this game with a partner.

What to do:
- Cut out the cards at the foot of the page.

- Place the cards face down on the table.

- Each player should take a card.

- The first player should:
  - use the spinner to find a mass in grams
  - toss the coin
  - add or subtract the spinner score to/from the amount on the card.

- The second pupil should repeat the steps, as above.

- The player who makes the greater mass scores a point.

- The winner is the first player to score 10 points.

How to use the spinner
Hold the paper clip in the centre of the spinner using the pencil and gently flick the paper clip with your finger to make it spin.

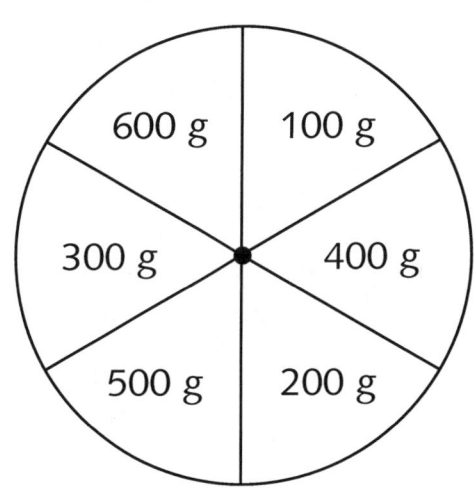

✂

1 kg	2 kg	3 kg
2 kg	900 g	900 g
1000 g	3000 g	

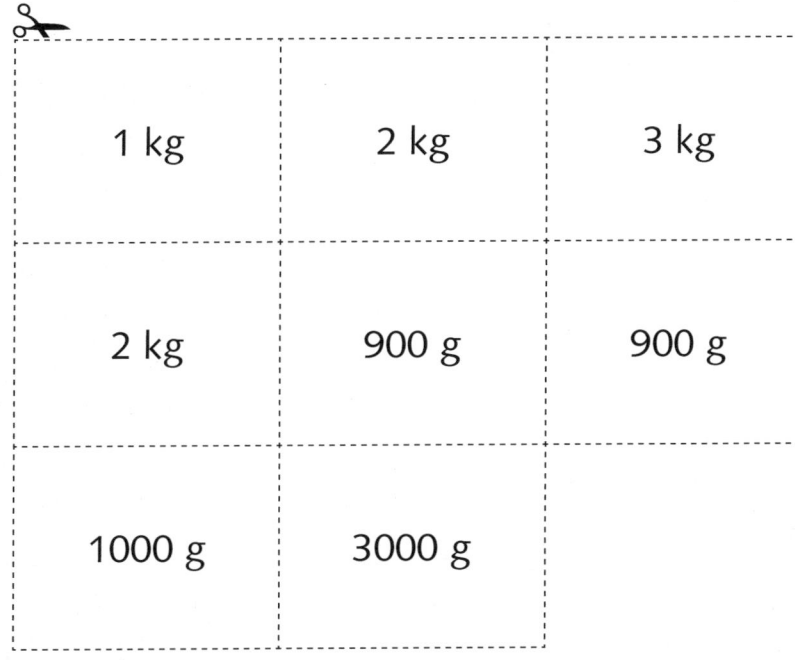

Spinner: 600 g, 100 g, 300 g, 400 g, 500 g, 200 g

Name: _____ Date: _____

Pick your own strawberries

Add and subtract masses

Six friends picked strawberries at a local fruit farm.
The farmer weighed their trays and they paid
for their fruit.

1 Complete the table for each tray of strawberries.

	John	Ellen	Hassan	Mina	Kayden	Lexi
Weight in grams						

2 Write which two trays together have a total mass of:

  a 5 kg: tray ⬚ + tray ⬚

  b 4 kg 500 g: tray ⬚ + tray ⬚

  c 5 kg 800 g: tray ⬚ + tray ⬚

3 Find the total mass of strawberries
picked by these children:

  a Ellen and Kayden ⬚

  b Hassan and Mina ⬚

4 Which three children together picked $7\frac{1}{2}$ kg
of strawberries?

⬚

5 On the way home John, Ellen and Hassan each ate
about 150 g of their strawberries. Find the mass of
strawberries left in each tray when they got home.

  a John ⬚   **b** Ellen ⬚   **c** Hassan ⬚

Scale (right side):
- 1 kg
- Lexi →
- 2 kg
- Kayden →
- Mina →
- Hassan →
- Ellen →
- 3 kg
- John →
- 4 kg

Name: _____ Date: _____

dding 1s

Add mentally a 3-digit number and 1s

Use the number line to work out these calculations.

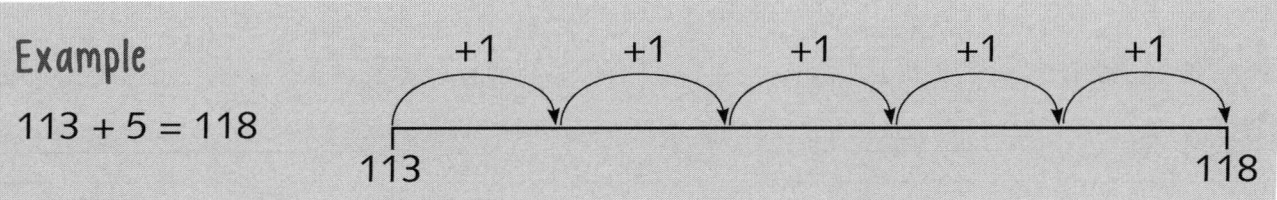

Example
113 + 5 = 118

+1 +1 +1 +1 +1

113   118

1 75 + 6 = [ ]

75

2 84 + 7 = [ ]

84

3 91 + 5 = [ ]

91

4 104 + 8 = [ ]

104

5 118 + 4 = [ ]

118

6 123 + 6 = [ ]

123

7 137 + 8 = [ ]

137

8 142 + 9 = [ ]

142

9 166 + 7 = [ ]

166

10 179 + 6 = [ ]

179

Name: _____ Date: _____

Missing numbers (1)

Add mentally, a 3-digit number and 10s

1 Solve these missing number calculations. Show your working out.

a [ ] + 60 = 251

b [ ] + 70 = 317

c [ ] + 40 = 472

d [ ] + 80 = 399

e [ ] + 60 = 573

f [ ] + 90 = 614

g [ ] + 50 = 748

h [ ] + 70 = 832

i [ ] + 40 = 901

j [ ] + 90 = 999

2 Explain how you worked out these missing number calculations.

_____

_____

_____

Name: _____ Date: _____

Counting on in 100s

Add mentally a 3-digit number and 100s

Practise counting on in 100s.

1

| 42 |
| 142 |
| 242 |
| |
| |
| |
| |
| |
| |
| 942 |

2

| 38 |
| |
| |
| |
| |
| |
| |
| |
| |
| 938 |

3

| 51 |
| |
| |
| |
| |
| |
| |
| |
| |
| |

4

| 49 |
| |
| |
| |
| |
| |
| |
| |
| |
| |

5

| 68 |
| |
| |
| |
| |
| |
| |
| |
| |
| |

6

| 77 |
| |
| |
| |
| |
| |
| |
| |
| |
| |

7

| 13 |
| |
| |
| |
| |
| |
| |
| |
| |
| |

8

| 94 |
| |
| |
| |
| |
| |
| |
| |
| |
| |

9

| 80 |
| |
| |
| |
| |
| |
| |
| |
| |
| |

10

| 99 |
| |
| |
| |
| |
| |
| |
| |
| |
| |

Name: _____ Date: _____

Shopping problems

Solve problems and reason mathematically

Crispy snacks 90 g

Cracker biscuits
143 g

Cheddar cheese
455 g

Chilli paste 50 g

Olives 268 g

Make up five word problems about the shop.
You can add in your own information.

Example

Kim went to the shop. She bought a pack of cheese and and some tomatoes. Her shopping weighed 700 g. How much did the tomatoes weigh?

1 _____

_____

2 _____

_____

3 _____

_____

4 _____

_____

5 _____

_____

Name: _____ **Date:** _____

Subtracting 1s

Subtract mentally a 3-digit number and 1s

Use the number line to work out these calculations.

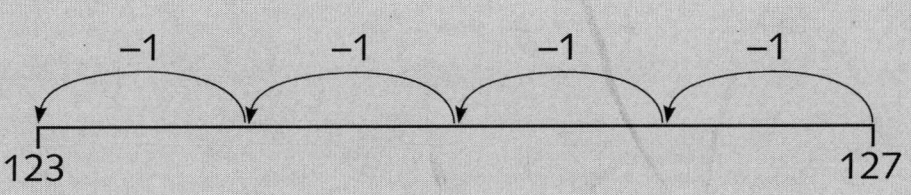

Example

$127 - 4 = 123$

-1 -1 -1 -1

123   127

1 $68 - 5 =$ [ ]

                             68

2 $72 - 4 =$ [ ]

                             72

3 $89 - 7 =$ [ ]

                             89

4 $115 - 6 =$ [ ]

                             115

5 $124 - 5 =$ [ ]

                             124

6 $137 - 6 =$ [ ]

                             137

7 $141 - 8 =$ [ ]

                             141

8 $155 - 9 =$ [ ]

                             155

9 $163 - 7 =$ [ ]

                             163

10 $184 - 8 =$ [ ]

                             184

Name: _____ Date: _____

Missing numbers (2)

Subtract mentally a 3-digit number and 10s

1 Solve these missing number calculations. Show your working out.

a [ ] $- 60 = 345$ **b** [ ] $- 40 = 421$

c [ ] $- 70 = 542$ **d** [ ] $- 50 = 499$

e [ ] $- 80 = 586$ **f** [ ] $- 30 = 678$

g [ ] $- 90 = 749$ **h** [ ] $- 40 = 866$

i [ ] $- 70 = 825$ **j** [ ] $- 80 = 903$

2 Explain how to work out these missing number calculations.

_____

_____

_____

Name: _____ Date: _____

ounting back in 100s

Subtract mentally a 3-digit number and 100s

Practise counting back in 100s.

1
| 915 |
| 815 |
| 715 |
| |
| |
| |
| |
| |
| |
| 15 |

2
| 962 |
| |
| |
| |
| |
| |
| |
| |
| |
| 62 |

3
| 981 |
| |
| |
| |
| |
| |
| |
| |
| |
| 81 |

4
| 933 |
| |
| |
| |
| |
| |
| |
| |
| |
| |

5
| 947 |
| |
| |
| |
| |
| |
| |
| |
| |
| |

6
| 963 |
| |
| |
| |
| |
| |
| |
| |
| |
| |

7
| 985 |
| |
| |
| |
| |
| |
| |
| |
| |
| |

8
| 980 |
| |
| |
| |
| |
| |
| |
| |
| |
| |

9
| 904 |
| |
| |
| |
| |
| |
| |
| |
| |
| |

10
| 977 |
| |
| |
| |
| |
| |
| |
| |
| |
| |

Name: _____ Date: _____

Swimming problems

Solve problems and reason mathematically

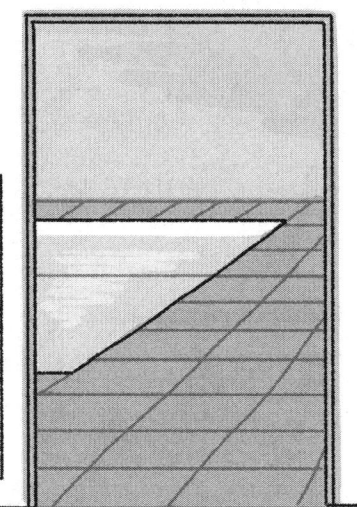

SWIMMING POOL

Child swim 35p
Adult swim 65p
The pool is 250 cm deep.
The pool is 60 metres long and 25 metres wide.
The pool opens at 9.00 a.m. every day
and closes at 6.00 p.m.

Make up five word problems about the pool. You can add in your own information.

Example

Lily went to the pool with her sister. They had £2. They both bought a ticket for swimming. How much money did they have left?

1 _____

_____

2 _____

_____

3 _____

_____

4 _____

_____

5 _____

_____

Name: _____ Date: _____

ore robot patterns

Make and describe right-angled turns

You will need:
• ruler

1 Repeat these robot patterns three more times.

a 1, 3, 4

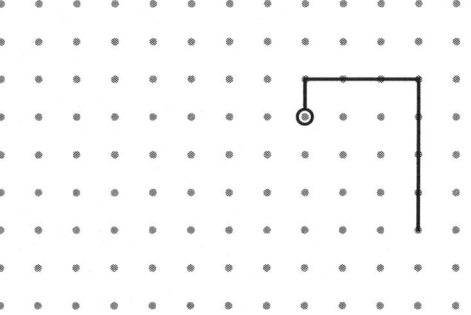

b 1, 3, 5

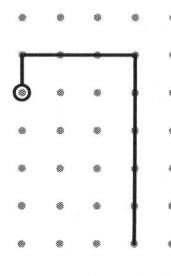

c 2, 3, 4

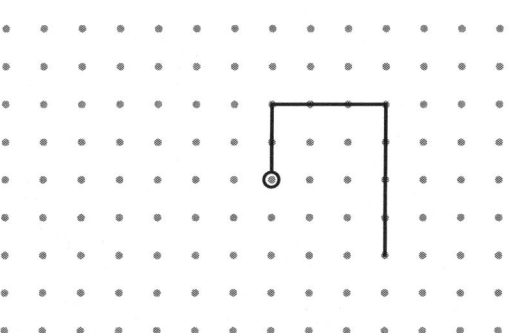

d 4, 3, 2

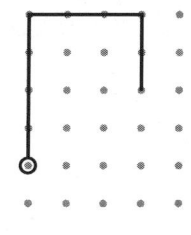

2 Write what you notice about the 2, 3, 4 and 4, 3, 2 pattern.

_____

_____

_____

Name: _____ Date: _____

Turning the hands

Give and follow instructions to make turns

You will need:
• right-angle tester

1 Write the number of right-angled turns made by the hour hand from:

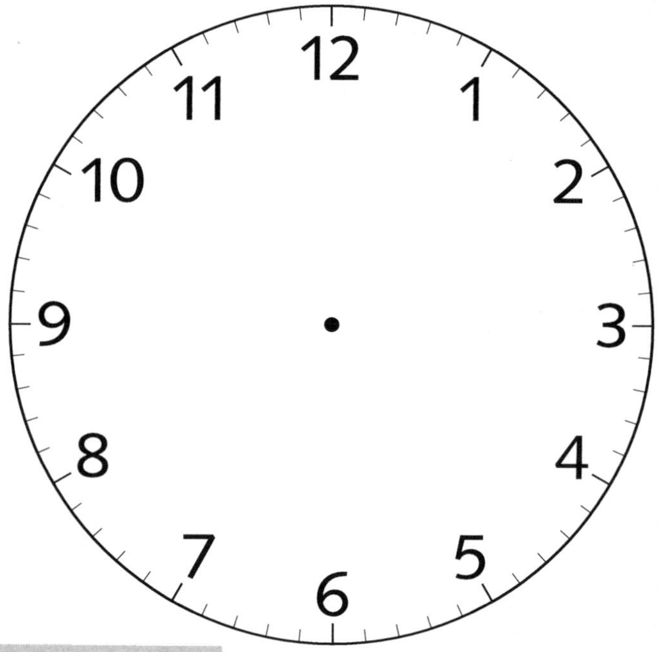

a 3 o'clock to 6 o'clock ☐

b 1 o'clock to 10 o'clock ☐

c 2 o'clock to 8 o'clock ☐

d 3 o'clock to 12 o'clock ☐

e 4 o'clock to 10 o'clock ☐

f 5 o'clock to 11 o'clock ☐

Hint Use your right-angle tester to help you.

2 Complete the table for these right-angled turns.

Starting time	Number of right-angled turns	Finishing time
a 3 o'clock	2 right-angled turns	☐ o'clock
b 8 o'clock	1 right-angled turn	☐ o'clock
c 2 o'clock	3 right-angled turns	☐ o'clock
d 5 o'clock	2 right-angled turns	☐ o'clock
e 12 o'clock	3 right-angled turns	☐ o'clock
f 9 o'clock	4 right-angled turns	☐ o'clock

Name: _____ Date: _____

Taking turns

Give and follow instructions to make turns

Play this game with a partner.

What to do:

• Take turns to:
  – place the pencil along a line and point to a letter
  – say the letter
  – spin the spinner.

• Your partner should guess which letter the pencil will point to after it turns, as shown by the spinner.

• Check the answer by turning the pencil.

• A correct answer wins 1 point. The winner is the first to score 10 points.

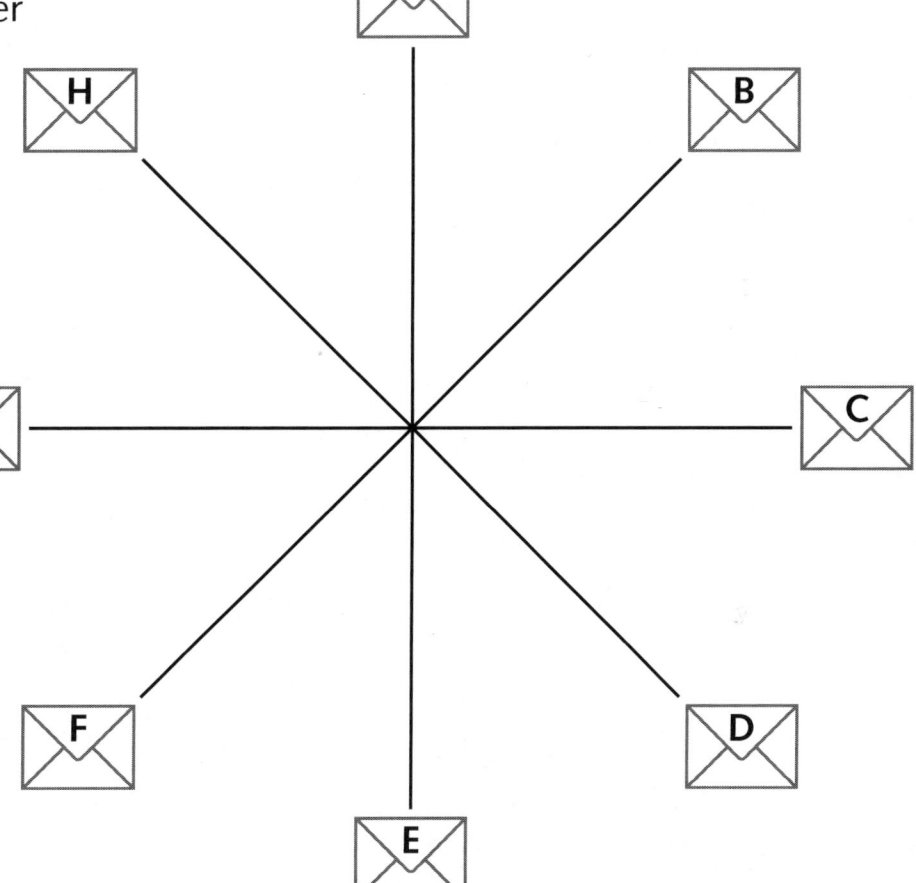

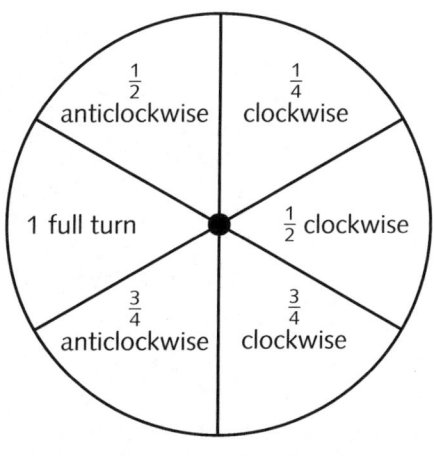

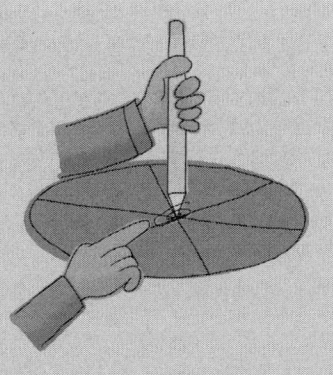

How to use the spinner

Hold the paper clip in the centre of the spinner using the pencil and gently flick the paper clip with your finger to make it spin.

Name: _____ Date: _____

All sorts of fans

Test whether an angle is greater than or less than a right angle

The handles of this fan make a right angle.

Use this fan to check the size of the other fans.

1 Carefully cut out all the fans.

2 Compare the fans to your right angle fan.

3 Draw this chart in your exercise book.
Use a whole page.

You will need:
- scissors
- glue

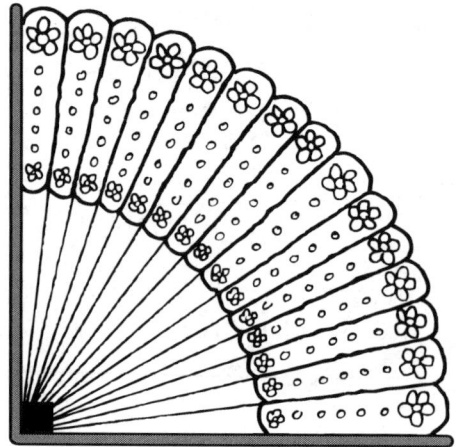

Less than a right angle	More than a right angle

4 Glue the fans in the correct column.

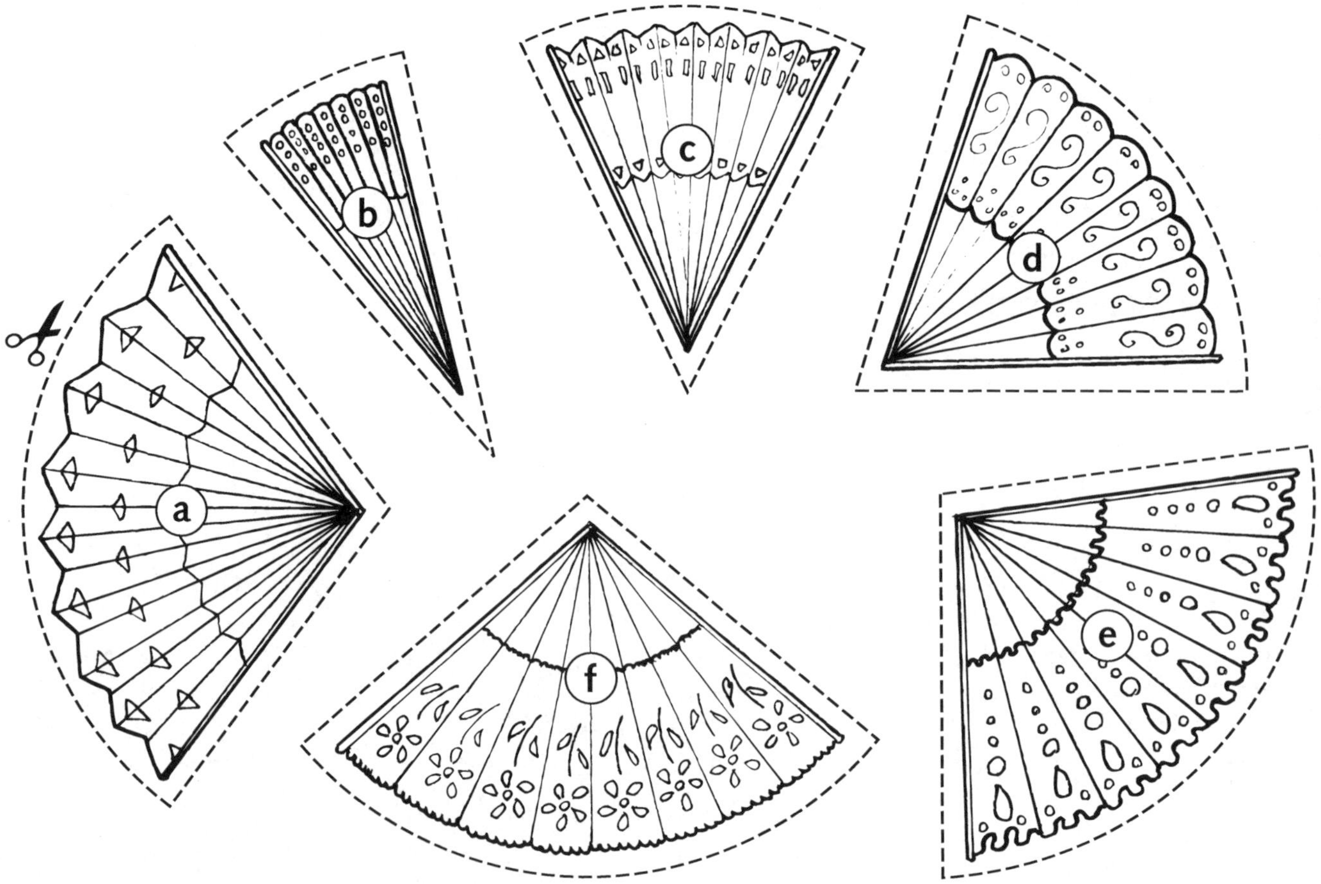

Name: _____ Date: _____

multiplication table

Recall the multiplication facts for the 4 multiplication table

Play this game with a partner.

What to do:

- Cover each number fact with a counter.

- Take turns to:
  – remove a counter
  – say the answer to the multiplication fact.

- Check the answer with your partner.

- If you are correct, keep the counter.
  If you are incorrect, place the counter
  back on the board.

- Continue until all the counters have been removed.

- The player with the most counters at the end is the winner.

4 × 6	4 × 12	7 × 4	11 × 4
5 × 4	4 × 8	4 × 4	4 × 5
10 × 4	1 × 4	4 × 9	12 × 4
9 × 4	6 × 4	3 × 4	2 × 4
8 × 4	4 × 7	4 × 4	4 × 3

Name: _____ Date: _____

Doubling to find the 4 multiplication table

Use doubling to recall the 4 multiplication table

1 Double the number each time.

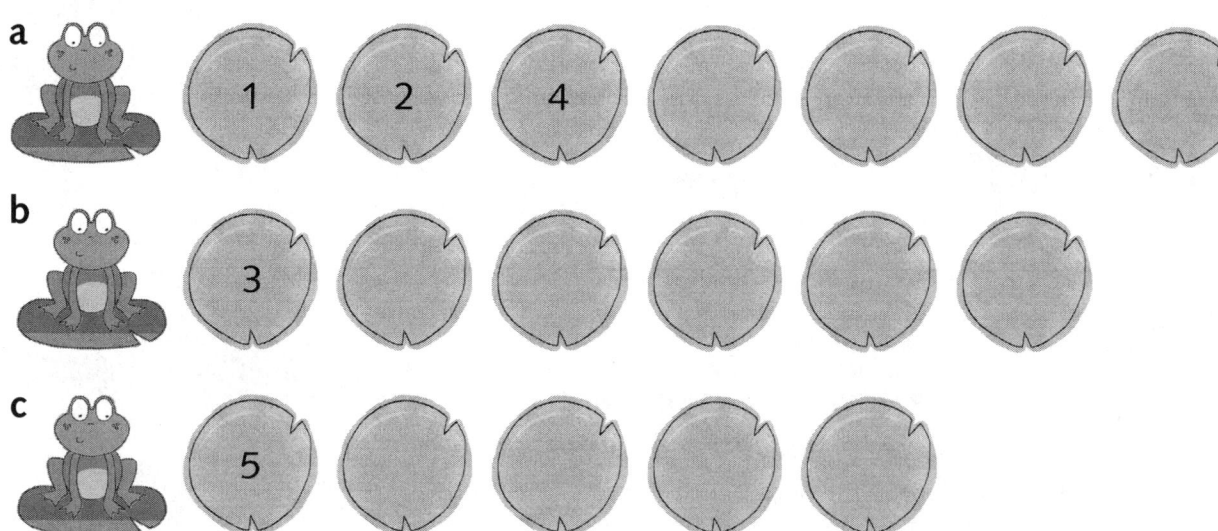

a 1 2 4

b 3

c 5

2 Look at the first array. Write the 2 multiplication fact.

Draw what you would see in the mirror image.
Write the 4 multiplication fact.

a

| $5 \times 2 = 10$ | $5 \times 4 = 20$ |

b

c

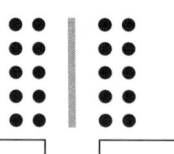

d

e

f

Name: _____ Date: _____

Speedy multiplication tables

- Use doubling to recall the 4 multiplication table
- Recall the multiplication facts for the 4 multiplication table

Play this game with a partner.

What to do:

- Take turns to:
  - roll the dice
  - write the number on your sheet to make a number fact
  - write the answer to the multiplication fact.

- Keep playing until you reach the end of the row. If you roll the same number twice you miss that turn.

- The player who reaches the end of the row first scores one point.

- The player with the most points after five games is the winner.

You will need:
- 1–12 dice

Game 1	☐ × 4 = ☐	4 × ☐ = ☐	☐ × 4 = ☐	4 × ☐ = ☐	4 × ☐ = ☐
Game 2	☐ = ☐ × 3	☐ × 3 = ☐	3 × ☐ = ☐	☐ = 3 × ☐	☐ × 3 = ☐
Game 3	☐ × 4 = ☐	4 × ☐ = ☐	☐ × 4 = ☐	4 × ☐ = ☐	4 × ☐ = ☐
Game 4	☐ = ☐ × 4	☐ × 4 = ☐	4 × ☐ = ☐	☐ = 4 × ☐	☐ × 4 = ☐
Game 5	3 × ☐ = ☐	4 × ☐ = ☐	☐ × 3 = ☐	☐ × 4 = ☐	5 × ☐ = ☐

Name: _____ Date: _____

Multiplication and division of 4

Write a multiplication statement that matches a division statement

Some of the numbers below have been multiplied by 4 and separated from their answer. Match them up and write the multiplication and division calculation for each.

Hint
Cross out each pair of numbers as you use them.

Example   60, 240 → 60 × 4 = 240 and 240 ÷ 4 = 60

×4

32   40   9   5   80   240   160   28   280   10

40   8   50   7   200   36   320   70   20   60

	Multiplication fact	Division fact
1	60 × 4 = 240	240 ÷ 4 = 60
2		
3		
4		
5		
6		
7		
8		
9		
10		

Name: _____ Date: _____

8 multiplication table

Recall the multiplication facts for the 8 multiplication table

Play this game with a partner.

What to do:

You will need:
• 20 counters

- Cover each number fact with a counter.

- Take turns to:
  - remove a counter
  - say the answer to the multiplication fact.

- Check the answer with your partner.

- If you are correct, keep the counter. If you are incorrect, place the counter back on the board.

- Continue until all the counters have been removed.

- The player with the most counters at the end is the winner.

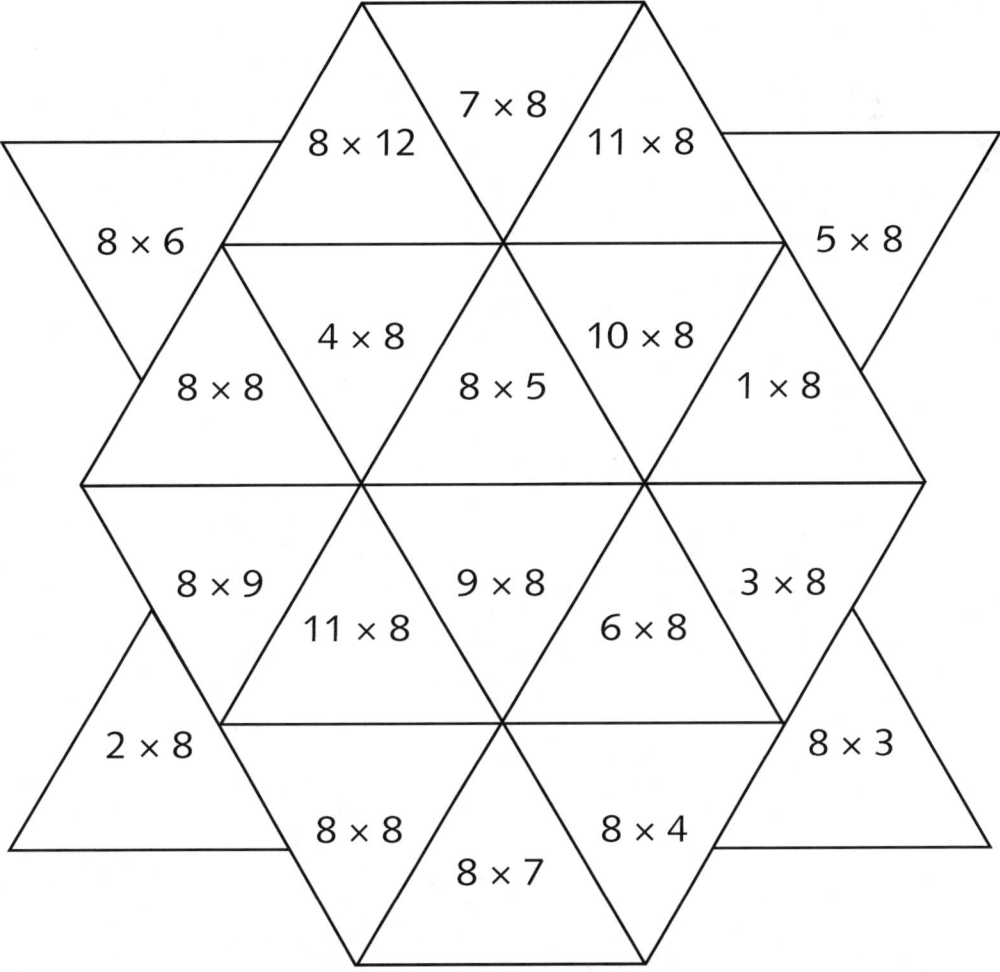

Name: _____ Date: _____

Doubling to find the 8 multiplication table

Use doubling to recall the 8 multiplication table

You will need:
• coloured pencil

1 Look at the first array. Write the 4 multiplication fact.

Draw what you see in the mirror image. Write the 8 multiplication fact.

a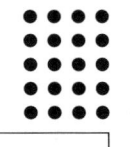

| 5 × 4 = 20 | | 5 × 8 = 40 |

b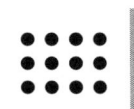

| | | |

c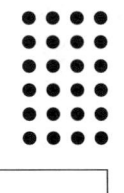

| | | |

d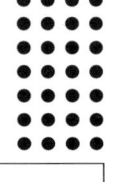

| | | |

e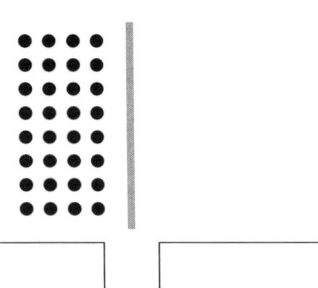

| | | |

f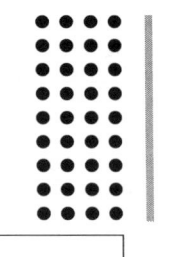

| | | |

2 Find and colour all the multiples of 8.

64   40   96   56   8

15   72   20   43

32   88

81

Name: _____ Date: _____

Doubling to find the 4 and 8 multiplication tables

Use known number facts to solve number problems

1 Find two numbers that multiply to give 24 and also add to make 11. ☐ ☐

2 Find two numbers that multiply to give 40 and also add to make 13. ☐ ☐

3 Find two numbers that multiply to give 24 and when subtracted give an answer of 2. ☐ ☐

4 Find two numbers that add to give 16 but when multiplied make a number 8 times larger than one of the numbers. ☐ ☐

5 Find two numbers that when subtracted give an answer of 4 but multiply to give 96. ☐ ☐

6 Find two numbers that when divided give an answer of 3 and when multiplied give an answer 4 times larger than one of the numbers. ☐ ☐

Name: _____ Date: _____

All things 8: solving word problems

Solve word problems

Each spider needs 8 pipe cleaners for the legs.

Year 3 made spiders in art and craft lessons. Write the calculation and answer to these questions.

| Example | $2 \times 8 = 16$ |

1 Each spider needs 8 pipe cleaners for the legs. Hatty made 3 spiders. How many pipe cleaners did she need?

2 Mary's group had a bag of 32 pipe cleaners on the table. How many spiders could be made? There are 6 children in the group. How many more pipe cleaners are needed so each child can make a spider?

3 The teacher placed 4 spiders on each web. There were 36 spiders in total. How many webs were needed?

4 There are 30 children in the Year 3 class. If they all made 1 spider each, how many pipe cleaners would they use?

5 In the class, all 30 children made 2 spiders and 20 of the children made an extra spider. How many pipe cleaners did they use?

6 In the class, all 30 children made 2 spiders and 20 of the children made an extra spider. Each of the spiders needed two plastic eyes. How many eyes were used altogether?

7 On the back of this sheet, make up your own spider story. Ask a friend to solve it.

Name: _____ Date: _____

Time to the minute

Tell and write the time to the minute on a 12-hour clock with hands

Draw the missing hands on the clock face and complete the missing time.

1

25 minutes to 3

2

☐ minutes ☐

3

15 minutes past 12

4

6 minutes to 8

5

☐ minutes ☐

6

☐ minutes ☐

7

22 minutes past 9

8

19 minutes to 2

9

☐ minutes ☐

10

☐ minutes ☐

Name: _____ Date: _____

Olympics time line

Use a time line and the vocabulary of time

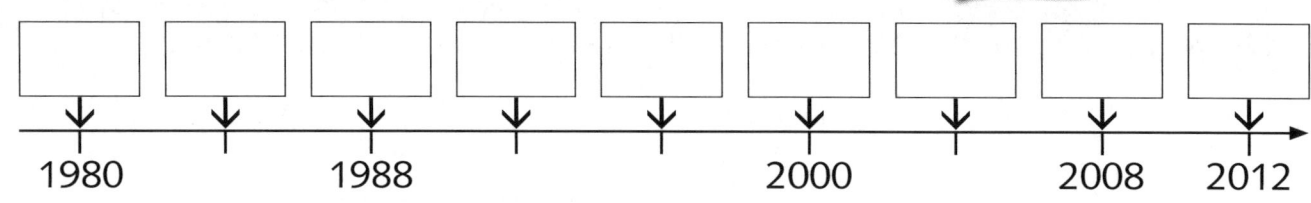

1980   1988   2000   2008   2012

1   Use the clues to work out the year in which each country held the summer Olympic Games. Write the letter or letters for the country above the correct year on the time line.

   a   London held the Olympic Games in 2012 [UK].

   b   In 2000 the Games were held in Australia [A].

   c   The Games were held in America [USA], first in Los Angeles in 1984 and 12 years later in Atlanta.

   d   China [C] held the Games after Greece [G] and before the UK.

   e   South Korea [SK] held the Games 4 years before Spain [S].

2   Find out who hosted the summer Olympic Games in 1980.

   _____

3   Find out the location of the Games in 2016.

   a   City _____ .   Country _____

   b   Draw the flag for that country.

4   Investigate where the last eight Winter Olympics were held.
   Draw a time line to show this on the back of this sheet.

Name: _____ Date: _____

Roman dials and station clocks

Read the time on a clock with Roman numerals
and on a 24-hour clock

1 Draw the missing hands on the clock face and complete the missing time.

a

15 minutes past [ ]

b

[ ] minutes to [ ]

c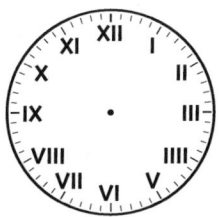

27 minutes past 11

d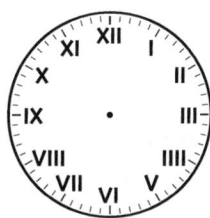

13 minutes to 4

2 Write the missing numbers in the
circles for the 24-hour clock.

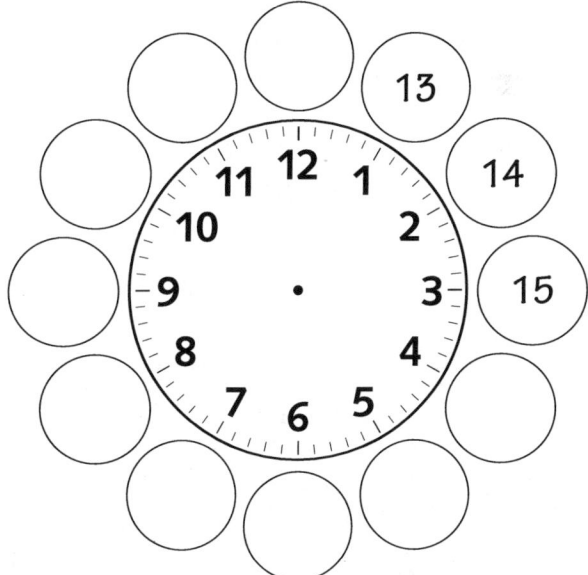

3 Circle the boxes below that show
the correct times.

Clock A
- In the evening.
- At 16 minutes past the hour.

Clock B
- In the afternoon.
- Earlier than 4 pm but later than
  half past 3.

| 6:50 | 9:16 | 18:16 |

| 15:30 | 4:50 | 15:40 |

Name: _____ Date: _____

Station times

Read the time to the minute on
12-hour and 24-hour clocks

The station clock shows 14:34.

1 Write the time the clock showed
for each of the following.

	24-hour clock	12-hour clock
a 5 minutes later		
b 20 minutes later		
c 10 minutes earlier		
d 30 minutes later		
e Half an hour ago		
f 3 hours ago		
g In 5 hours' time		

2 Peter arrived at the station just after 2:30 p.m.
  • The station clock showed 14:34.
  • His train for Inverness leaves at 14:50.
How many minutes did he have to board his train? ☐

3 Complete the table for these train departures.

Destination	Train departs	
	12-hour clock	24-hour clock
a Glasgow	11:53 a.m.	
b Perth		12:22
c Aberdeen	3:10 p.m.	
d Newcastle		18:45
e London	10:05 p.m.	

Name: _____ Date: _____

Making 3-digit numbers

Recognise the place value of each digit in a 3-digit number

You will need:
• Base 10 material

- Write a 3-digit number in the circles below.

- Use the Base 10 materials to make your number.

- Put them in the correct columns.

- Record your number in the boxes below.

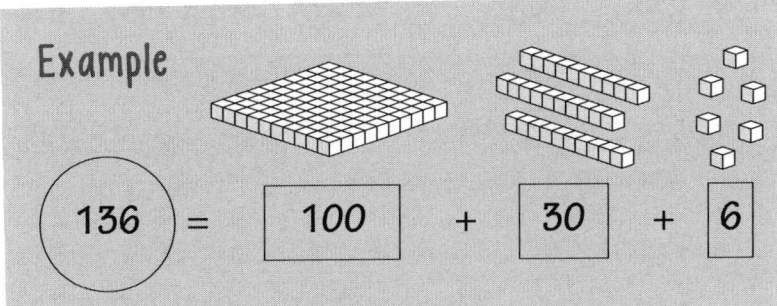

Example

$136 = 100 + 30 + 6$

100s	10s	1s

◯ = [ ] + [ ] + [ ]   ◯ = [ ] + [ ] + [ ]

◯ = [ ] + [ ] + [ ]   ◯ = [ ] + [ ] + [ ]

◯ = [ ] + [ ] + [ ]   ◯ = [ ] + [ ] + [ ]

◯ = [ ] + [ ] + [ ]   ◯ = [ ] + [ ] + [ ]

◯ = [ ] + [ ] + [ ]   ◯ = [ ] + [ ] + [ ]

Name: _____ Date: _____

Larger number wins

Recognise the place value of each digit in a 3-digit number

Play this game with a partner.

You will need:
- 0–9 digit cards
- 20 counters

- Before you start, shuffle the cards and place them face down in a pile.

- Look at the place value table below and choose 100s, 10s or 1s.

- Turn over a digit card and put it in your chosen column. Once you have placed your card, it cannot be changed.

- Repeat until all the columns are full, then the player with the larger number takes a counter.

- The first player to get 10 counters is the winner.

100s	10s	1s

Name: _____ Date: _____

How much money?

Represent and estimate numbers using money

Work with a partner.

- Talk to your partner and together, write two suggestions for good estimating.

What makes good estimating?

1 _____

_____

2 _____

_____

- Take turns to:
  - take a small handful of coins from the bag (making sure to keep them secret)
  - put the coins on the table, count to five and cover up the coins
  - ask your partner to write an estimate of the amount in pence.

You will need:
- bag of £1, 10p and 1p coins

- Record your estimates and actual amounts in the table.

- Check together how close each estimate is.

Estimate	Actual amount

Name: _____ Date: _____

Find your way

Compare and order numbers up to 100

1 Find a way from Start to End by drawing lines to join the numbers.

A line can go sideways ← →, up and down ↑ ↓, or diagonally ↗↖↘↙.

Your numbers must be in order, smallest to largest.

If you come to an empty square, you can write any number in it, as long as your numbers stay in order.

Start	27	39	43	30
	32	49		28
66	53	38	62	
55	60		61	
83		59		End

2 Now find a different way from Start to End.

Start	27	39	43	30
	32	49		28
66	53	38	62	
55	60		61	
83		59		End

Name: _____ Date: _____

Amounts of money

Add amounts of money

You will need:
- selection of
  1p, 2p, 5p, 10p,
  20p and 50p coins
  (per child)

- Using the coins, make the amounts of money.

- Use as few coins as possible.

- Write down the coins you use as an addition calculation.

Example

78p = (50p) + (20p) + (5p) + (2p) + (1p) + ( ) + ( ) + ( )

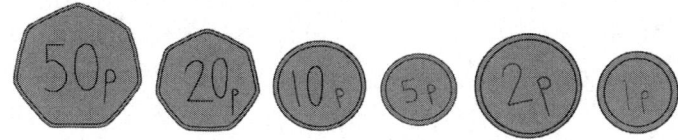

- Only fill in the circles that you need.

1 14p = ( ) + ( ) + ( ) + ( ) + ( ) + ( ) + ( ) + ( )

2 28p = ( ) + ( ) + ( ) + ( ) + ( ) + ( ) + ( ) + ( )

3 35p = ( ) + ( ) + ( ) + ( ) + ( ) + ( ) + ( ) + ( )

4 43p = ( ) + ( ) + ( ) + ( ) + ( ) + ( ) + ( ) + ( )

5 72p = ( ) + ( ) + ( ) + ( ) + ( ) + ( ) + ( ) + ( )

6 65p = ( ) + ( ) + ( ) + ( ) + ( ) + ( ) + ( ) + ( )

7 57p = ( ) + ( ) + ( ) + ( ) + ( ) + ( ) + ( ) + ( )

Name: _____ Date: _____

How much change?

Subtract amounts of money to give change

Fred goes into a café. He has £2 (200p). There are six items on the menu, each with a different price. Work out the different amounts of change he will get when Fred buys combinations of items from the menu. Remember to show your working out.

MENU

Ice cream £1·05

Juice 42p

Cheese and tomato sandwich 94p

Tuna sandwich 85p

Piece of carrot cake 57p

Banana 70p

1 How much change will Fred get if he buys:

a a tuna sandwich and a juice?

b a cheese and tomato sandwich and a piece of carrot cake?

c a tuna sandwich and a banana?

d a juice and an ice cream?

e a cheese and tomato sandwich and a banana?

f a banana and a piece of carrot cake?

Working out

2 Fred's friend Philippe buys three items. He pays for them with a £2 coin and receives 16p in change. What three items did he buy?

_____

Name: _____ Date: _____

Calculating change

Subtract amounts of money to give change

Work out the change if you buy this fruit.
You have 50p to spend each time.

Example

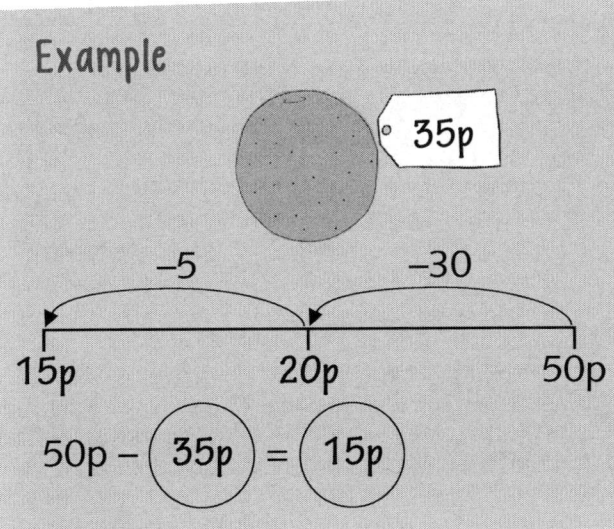

$$50p - \left(35p\right) = \left(15p\right)$$

1

$$50p - \bigcirc = \bigcirc$$

2

$$50p - \bigcirc = \bigcirc$$

3

$$50p - \bigcirc = \bigcirc$$

4

$$50p - \bigcirc = \bigcirc$$

5 30p

$$50p - \bigcirc = \bigcirc$$

Name: _____ Date: _____

Furniture shop

Write word problems involving money

Make up your own problems about the children in the furniture shop.

You must work them out so you know the answer!

1

2

3

4

5

Name: _____ **Date:** _____

New shapes from old

Solve problems involving shape

- Cut out one square at the bottom of this sheet.

- Cut along the dotted line to make two shapes.

- Join the two shapes along matching sides
  to make a new shape.

- Stick the shape on to this sheet.

- Circle the right angles with a red pencil.
  Make three more shapes in this way.

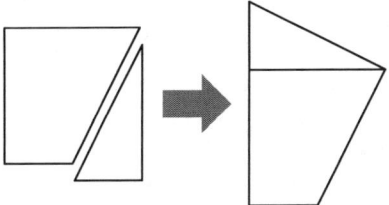

Shape 1

Shape 2

Shape 3

Shape 4

Name: _____ Date: _____

Triangles in a row

Describe patterns to solve a problem

You will need:
• ruler

1 Work out how these triangles get bigger each time.

Draw the next three triangles in the pattern.

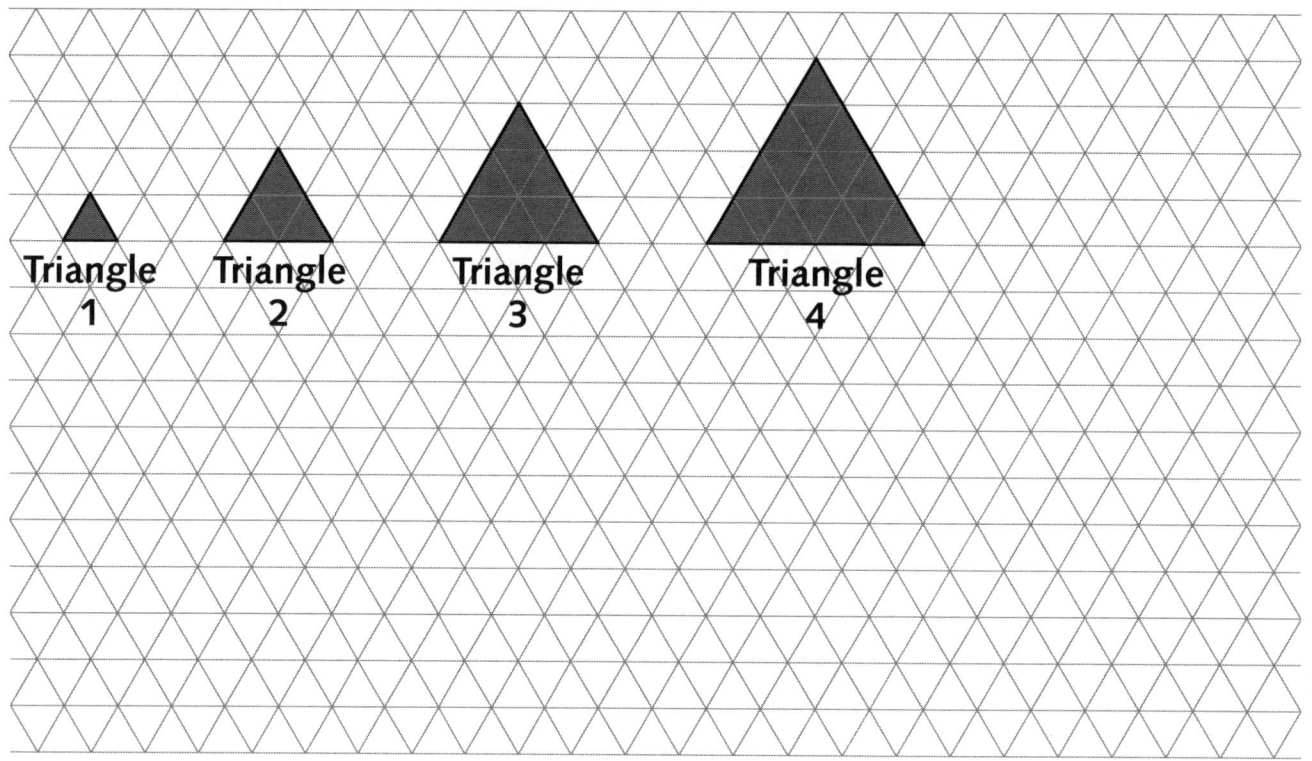

2 Complete the table for seven triangles. Two are done for you,

Triangle	1	2	3	4	5	6	7
Number of small triangles	1	4					

3 Write what you notice about the pattern for the number of small triangles.

_____

_____

4 Predict the number of small triangles for:

   a Triangle 8 [ ]   **b** Triangle 10 [ ]

Name: _____ Date: _____

Exploring shapes

Make shapes using folding and cutting

Shape 1

- Cut out the four triangles and the square.

- Fit them together to make a 4-pointed shape.

Shape 2

Cut out the six triangles.

Fit them together to make a 6-pointed shape.

Shape 1

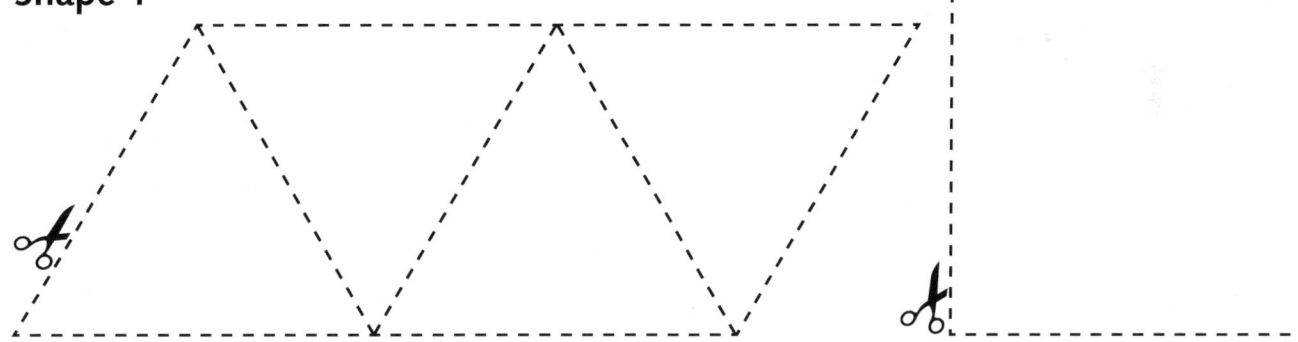

Shape 2

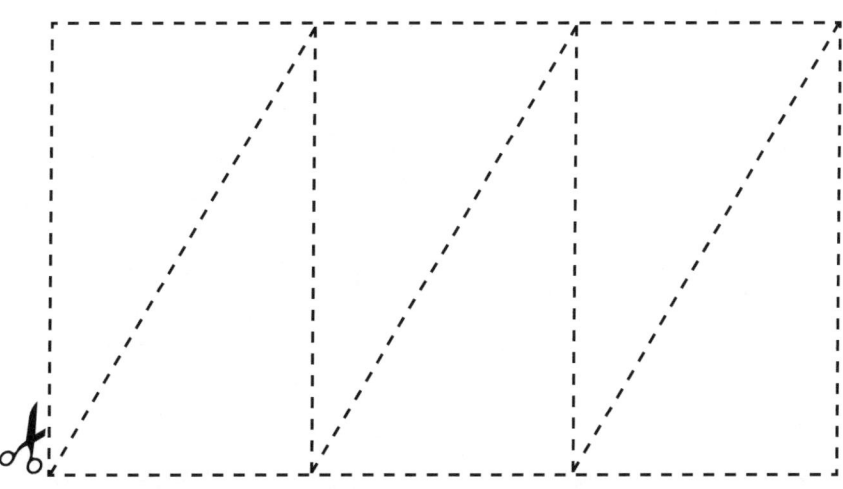

Name: _____ Date: _____

Exploring shapes

Make shapes using folding and cutting

1 Cut out the three triangles.

Cut each triangle in half.

Use the six pieces
to make a
6-pointed shape.

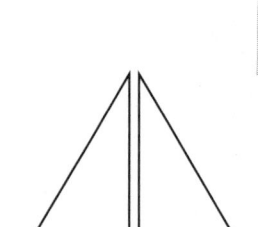

2 Cut out the four squares.

Cut each square in half.

Use the eight pieces to make
an 8-pointed shape.

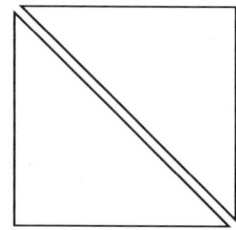

3 Cut out the four triangles. What if you cut
each equilateral triangle in a different way?

How many points do you think your
shape will have? Make your shape.

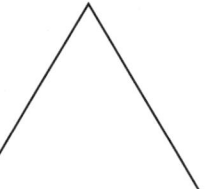
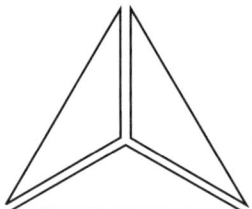

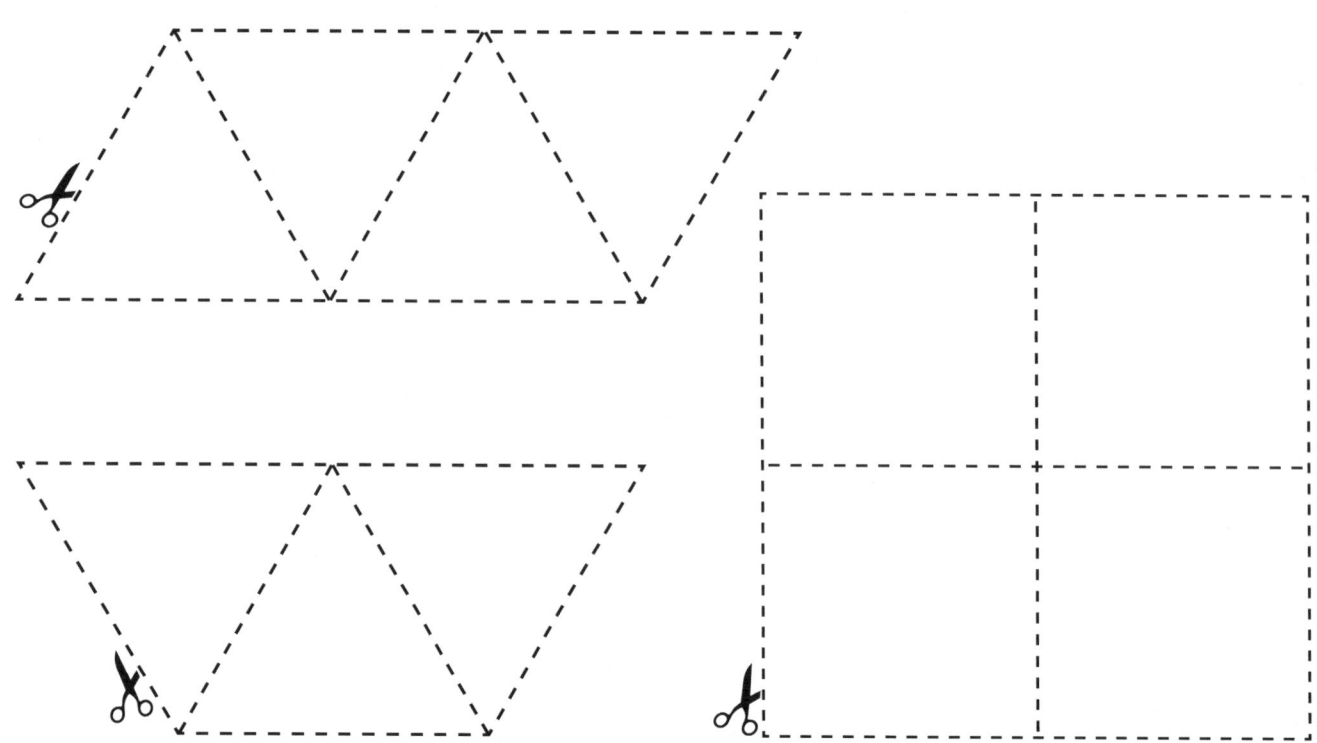

Name: _____ Date: _____

Counting in steps of 2, 4 and 8

Count in multiples of 2, 4 and 8

You will need:
• coloured pencils

1 Find and colour the multiples of each number.

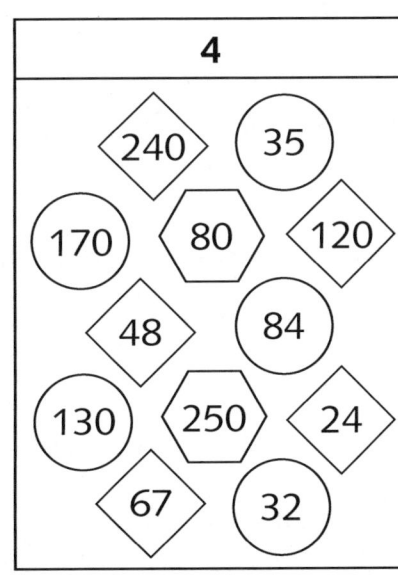

2
100 76
44 93 58
120 111
92 87 46
37 60

4
240 35
170 80 120
48 84
130 250 24
67 32

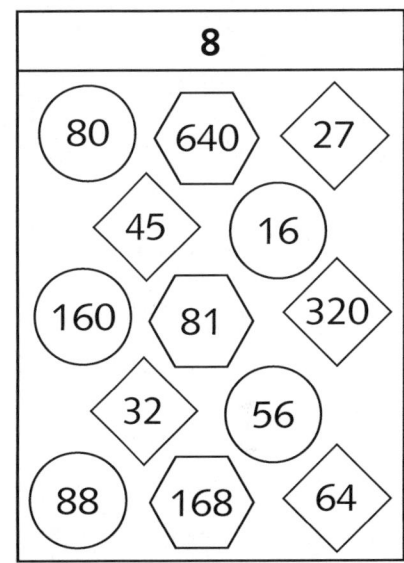

8
80 640 27
45 16
160 81 320
32 56
88 168 64

2 Write each missing number in the correct position on the number lines.

a 60 ———————————————————————— 84

b 24 ————— 40 ———————————————— 72

c 24 ———————————————— 80 ———— 120

d 0 40 —————————————————————— 480

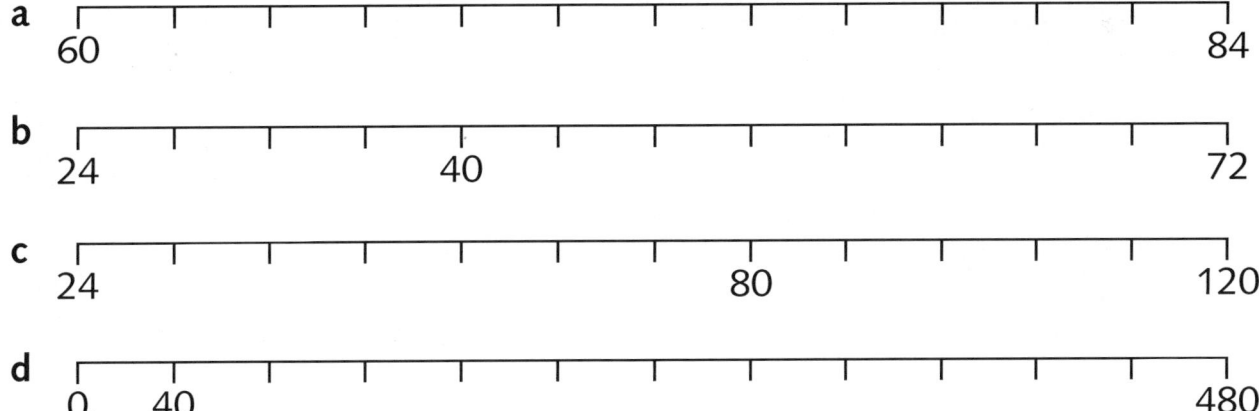

3 Fill in the missing multiples of each start number.

a 40, ☐, ☐, 160, ☐, ☐, ☐, ☐, ☐, 400, ☐, ☐

b 20, ☐, 60, ☐, ☐, ☐, ☐, ☐, 200, ☐, ☐

c 80, ☐, ☐, ☐, 400, ☐, ☐, ☐, ☐, ☐, 880,

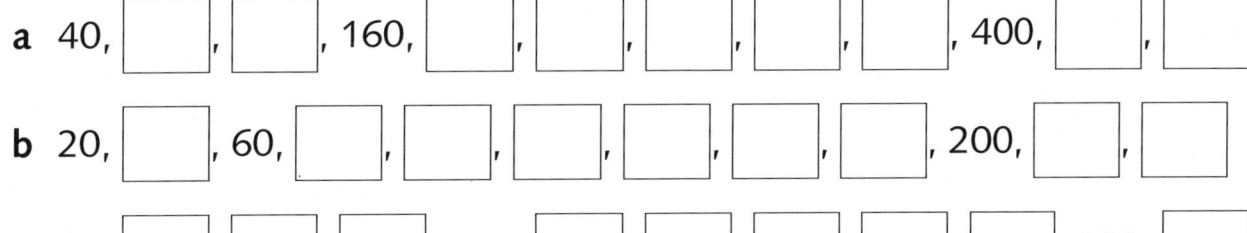

Name: _____ Date: _____

Halving to find division facts (1)

Use halving to recall the division facts for the 4 multiplication table

1 Find and colour the multiples of 4.

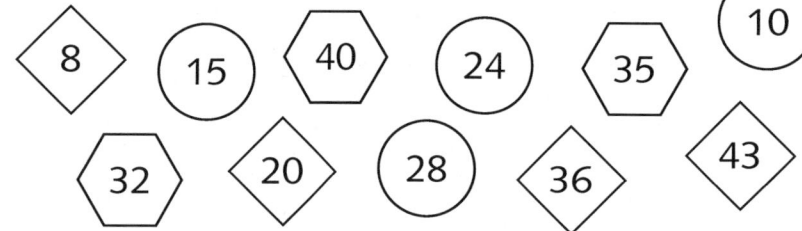

You will need:
• coloured pencils

2 • Write the total number of stamps under each array.

• The post office worker sells half. Write how many are left. She sells half again. Write how many are left.

• Write a division fact for each array using the 4 multiplication table.

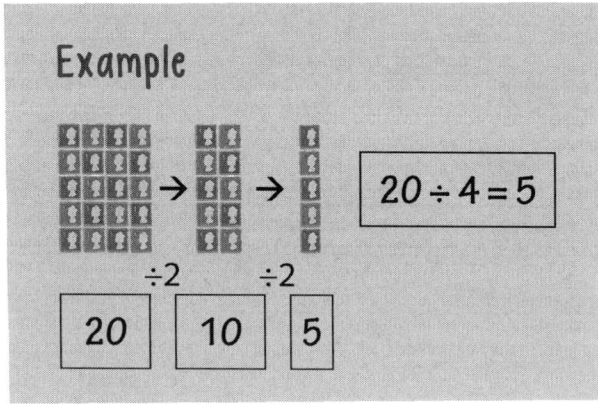

Example

$20 \div 4 = 5$

÷2 ÷2
| 20 | 10 | 5 |

a

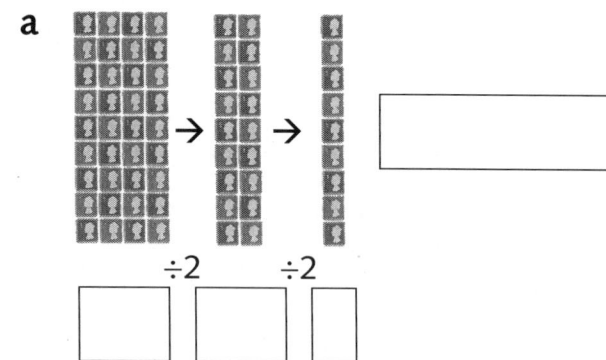

÷2 ÷2

b

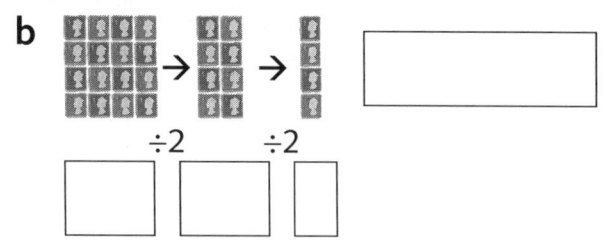

÷2 ÷2

c

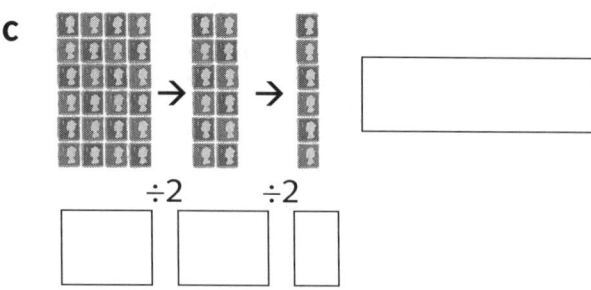

÷2 ÷2

d

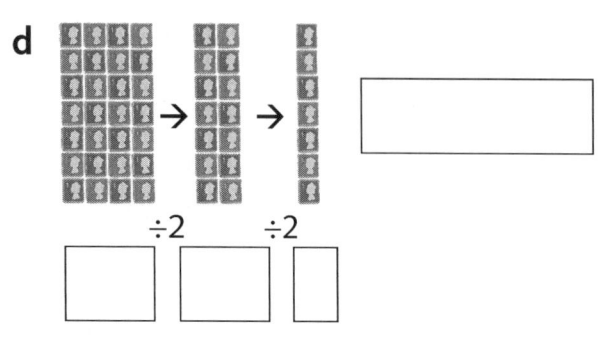

÷2 ÷2

e

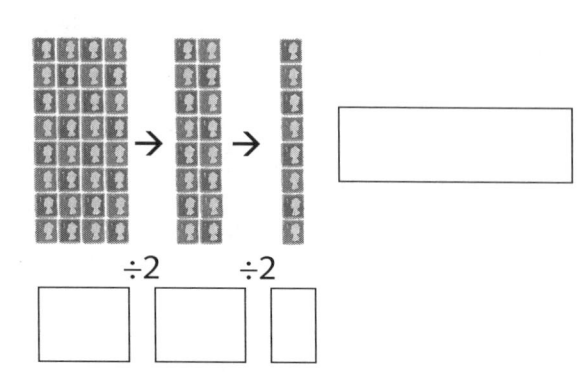

÷2 ÷2

Name: _____ Date: _____

lalving to find division facts (2)

Use halving to recall the division facts for the 8 multiplication table

- Write the total number of chocolate pieces under each array.

- Share half. Write how many are left. Share another half. Write how many are left. Share half again. Write how many are remaining.

- Write a division fact for each array using the 8 multiplication table.

Example

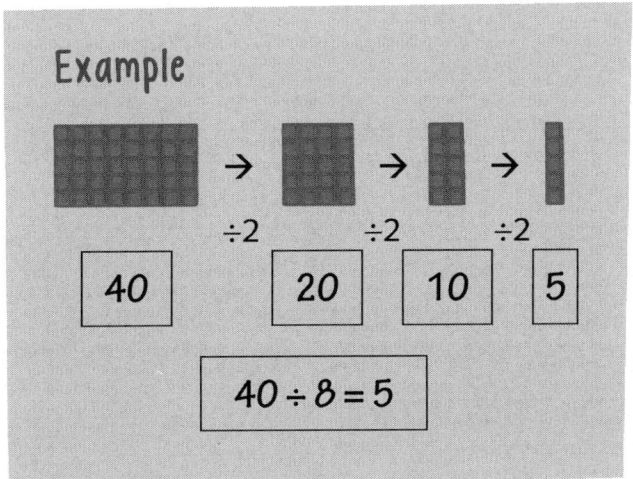

| 40 | ÷2 | 20 | 10 | ÷2 | 5 |

40 ÷ 8 = 5

1

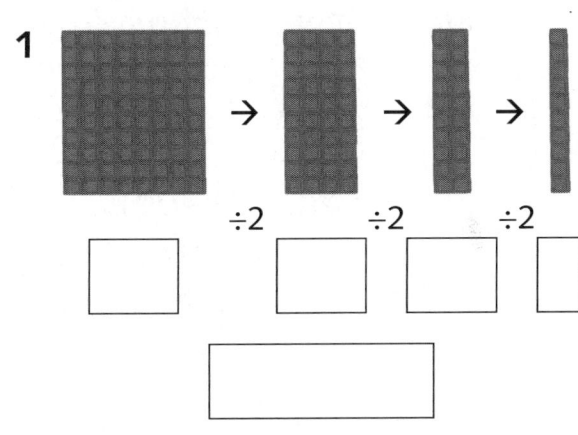

2

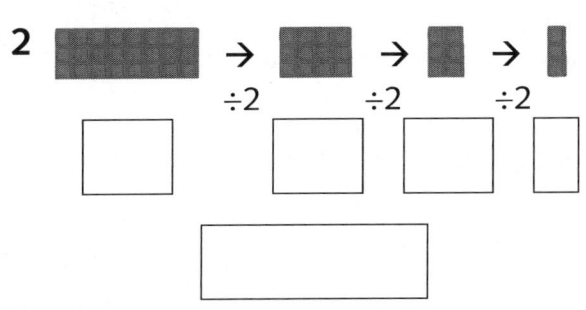

3

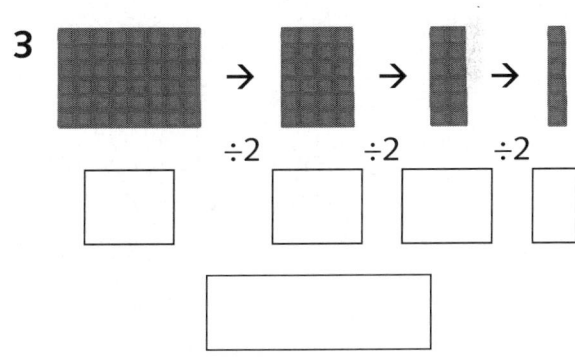

4

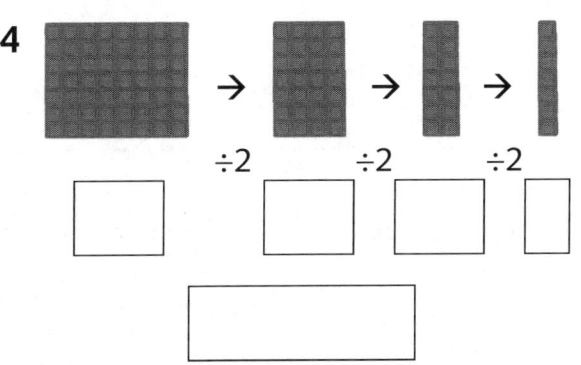

5

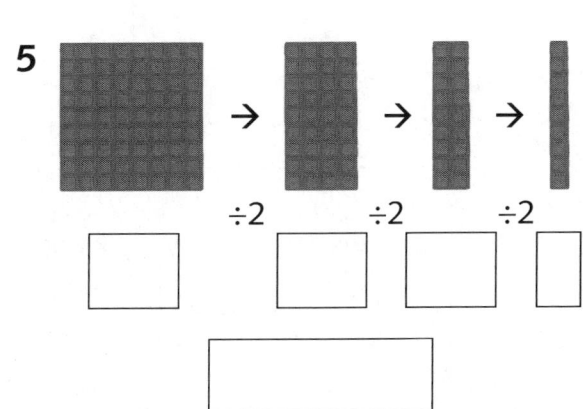

Name: _____ Date: _____

Solving word problems

Solve word problems and reason mathematically

 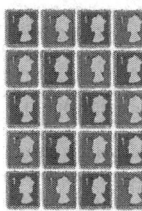 

1 The Post Office sells stamps in arrays. Read each question below and decide which operation to use. Write the calculation and then write the answer to the problem.

a A sheet of stamps has 64 stamps altogether. There are eight rows of stamps. How many stamps in each row? ☐	**b** A sheet of stamps has 64 stamps altogether. There are eight rows of stamps. Nasima buys three rows of stamps. How many stamps does she buy altogether? ☐
c A sheet of stamps has 64 stamps altogether. There are eight rows of stamps. Nadia buys six rows of stamps. How many stamps are left? ☐	**d** Stamps are sold in separate packs of 24 stamps and 40 stamps. Robin buys two packs of each. How many stamps does Robin have altogether? ☐

2 Make up your own word problem about stamps for these calculations and write them on the back of this sheet.

a $72 \div 8 = $ ☐   b $6 \times 8 = $ ☐   c $(4 \times 6) + 2 = $ ☐

Name: _____ Date: _____

Finding quarters

Divide objects into quarters

You will need:
• 28 counters

$\frac{1}{4}$ $\frac{1}{4}$

$\frac{1}{4}$ $\frac{1}{4}$

- Use the number of counters below.
- Divide the counters equally into quarters using the tray.
- Count how many counters are in each quarter.
- Fill in each answer.

1 8 counters $\frac{1}{4}$ = ☐   **2** 12 counters $\frac{1}{4}$ = ☐

3 20 counters $\frac{1}{4}$ = ☐   **4** 28 counters $\frac{1}{4}$ = ☐

5 16 counters $\frac{1}{4}$ = ☐   **6** 24 counters $\frac{1}{4}$ = ☐

Explain what you do to find $\frac{1}{4}$ of a set of counters.

_____

_____

_____

Name: _____ Date: _____

Non-unit fractions

Find non-unit fractions of amounts

Find the unit fraction of each amount.

Use this to find the non-unit fraction.

1 $\frac{2}{3}$ of 18

2 $\frac{2}{5}$ of 10

3 $\frac{3}{5}$ of 20

4 $\frac{2}{4}$ of 16

5 $\frac{2}{6}$ of 12

6 $\frac{4}{6}$ of 24

7 $\frac{3}{5}$ of 40

8 $\frac{4}{7}$ of 21

Name: _____ Date: _____

Fraction diagrams

Compare and order unit fractions

You will need:
• ruler

1 Draw a diagram to show each of these fractions.

Use a ruler to make sure your diagrams are clear and accurate.

a $\frac{1}{4}$

b $\frac{1}{3}$

c $\frac{1}{8}$

d $\frac{1}{6}$

e $\frac{1}{10}$

f $\frac{1}{7}$

2 Write the 6 fractions from Question 1 in order, smallest to largest.

☐ , ☐ , ☐ , ☐ , ☐ , ☐

3 How do diagrams help to compare and order fractions?

_____

_____

Name: _____ Date: _____

Shading number lines

Write fractions on number lines

You will need:
• coloured pencils

1 This rectangle is divided in half. It has two equal parts.

   a Shade both parts different colours.

   b Write 0, $\frac{1}{2}$, 1 on the number line.

2 This rectangle is divided into quarters. It has four equal parts.

   a Shade the parts different colours.

   b Write 0, $\frac{1}{4}$, $\frac{2}{4}$, $\frac{3}{4}$, 1 on the number line.

3 This rectangle is divided into thirds. It has three equal parts.

   a Shade the parts different colours.

   b Write 0, $\frac{1}{3}$, $\frac{2}{3}$, 1 on the number line.

4 This rectangle is divided into sixths. It has six equal parts.

   a Shade the parts different colours.

   b Write 0, $\frac{1}{6}$, $\frac{2}{6}$, $\frac{3}{6}$, $\frac{4}{6}$, $\frac{5}{6}$, 1 on the number line.

Name: _____ Date: _____

Millimetres of bracelets

Use a ruler to measure lines to the
nearest millimetre

You will need:
• ruler

1 Estimate, then measure, the
length of each bracelet to the
nearest whole centimetre.

Length of bracelet	
Estimate in cm	Measure in cm
a	
b	
c	
d	
e	

2 Estimate, then measure, the
length of each bracelet to the
nearest millimetre.

Length of bracelet	
Estimate in mm	Measure in mm
a	
b	
c	
d	
e	

a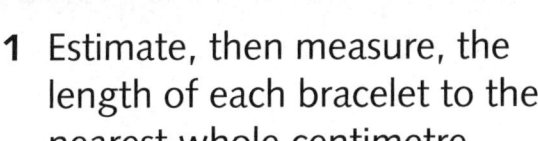

b

c

d

e

Remember to
include the
fastenings at
the ends.

Name: _____ Date: _____

Spirals in millimetres

Use a ruler to draw and measure lines
to the nearest millimetre

You will need:
• ruler

1 a This spiral increases by 5 mm on each new side.
Continue the spiral as far as you can go.

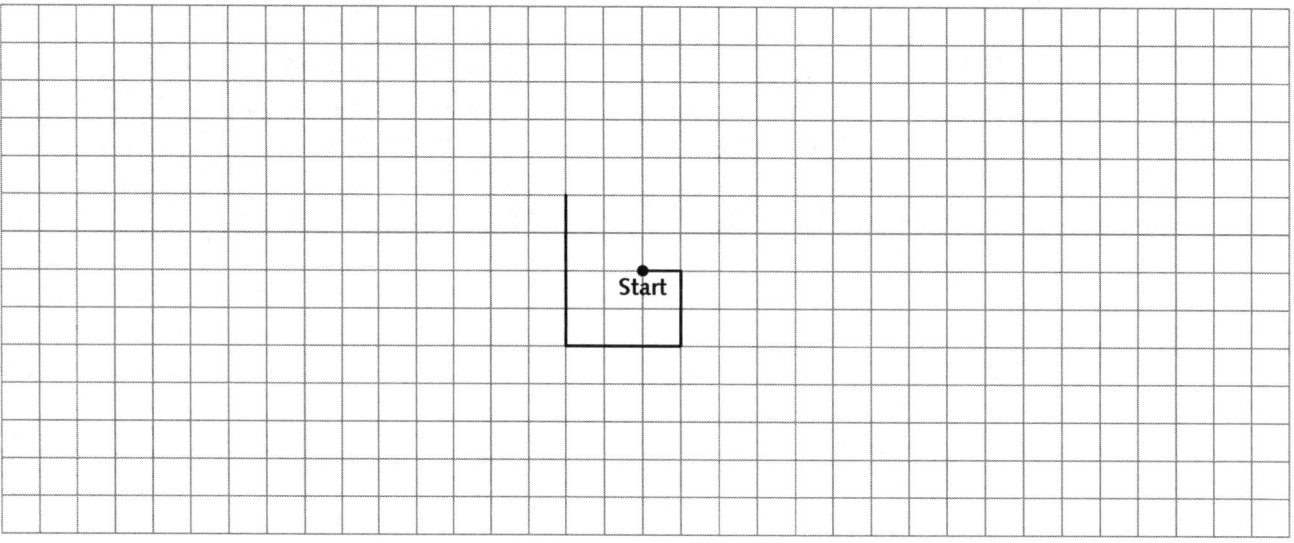

b Find the total length of your spiral.

My spiral measures ☐ cm altogether.

2 a Continue this spiral on the 5 mm triangular paper as far as you can go.

b Find the total length of your spiral.

My spiral measures ☐ cm altogether.

Name: _____ Date: _____

Comparing lengths

Use rulers to measure and compare lengths

1 Work with a partner.

a Collect about ten different objects.

Here are some ideas.

glue stick	paintbrush	felt-tip pen	coloured pencil	eraser
box	crayon	shoe	lunchbox	tin	paper clip	scissors

b Compare the length of each item against the strips at the bottom of the sheet.

c Write the name of each item in the correct place in the table.

Shorter than 10 cm	Between 10 cm and 15 cm long	Longer than 15 cm

10 cm

15 cm

Name: _____ Date: _____

Skateboard jumps

Compare lengths and use scaling of lengths

Children took part in the Finals of the Skateboard Jumping Competition.

1 Look at the results board. Work out which skateboarder jumped these distances.

a Just over $1\frac{1}{2}$ m.

b 1 m less than Skateboarder E.

c 1 m more than Skateboarder E.

d 2 m less than Skateboarder F.

e 50 cm less than Skateboarder F.

f Twice as far as Skateboarder D.

g Three times as far as Skateboarder B.

h Five times as far as Skateboarder A.

2 By how many centimetres did the winner beat:

a the runner-up? ☐ cm

b the competitor who came third? ☐ cm

3 Write three statements comparing the results for pairs of skateboarders.

_____

_____

_____

Name: _____ Date: _____

Adding 1s and 10s

Add 2-digit numbers using the expanded
written method of column addition

Add these 2-digit numbers
using the expanded method.
Practising with 2-digit
numbers will help you learn
the method.

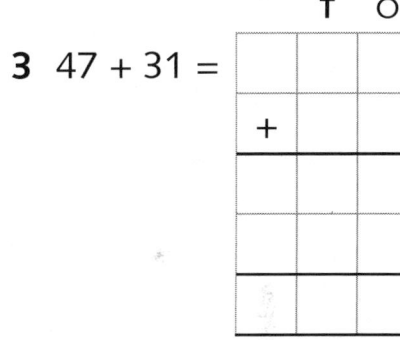

Example

	T	O	
$26 + 52 =$	2	6	
+	5	2	
		8	1s add 1s
	7	0	**10s** add **10s**
	7	8	**10s** add 1s

1 $36 + 45 =$

2 $24 + 43 =$

3 $47 + 31 =$

4 $54 + 25 =$

5 $48 + 51 =$

6 $72 + 26 =$

7 $39 + 50 =$

8 $42 + 57 =$

9 $82 + 15 =$

Name: _____ Date: _____

Addition instructions

Add 3-digit numbers using the formal written method
of column addition

1 Write a set of instructions for using the column method of addition.

When you have written the instructions, ask a partner to use them.

_____

_____

_____

_____

_____

_____

_____

_____

_____

_____

2 Addition puzzle

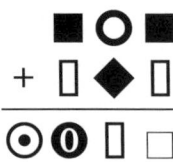

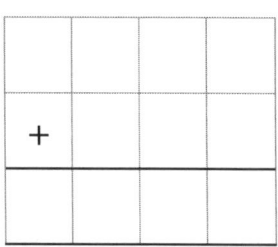

Working out

Each symbol stands for a different digit.
Work out which digit each letter
stands for to do the calculation.

Hint ☐ = 9 and **O** = 7.

Name: _____ Date: _____

Addition puzzle

Add 3-digit numbers using the formal written method of column addition

1 Using the digits 1, 2, 3, 4, 5 and 6, make up as many different addition calculations as you can.

2 Work out the answers below.

3 Check your answers with a partner. Have they found any different answers to yours?

I have used all the digits from 1 to 6. Now I can work out the answer.

	H	T	O
	2	5	6
+	1	3	4

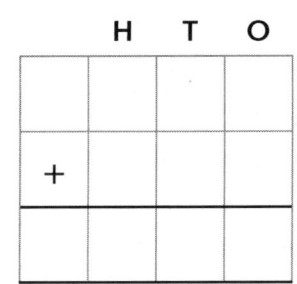
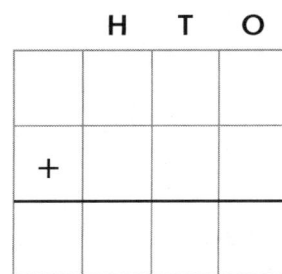
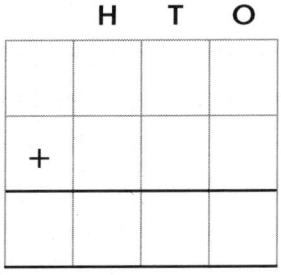
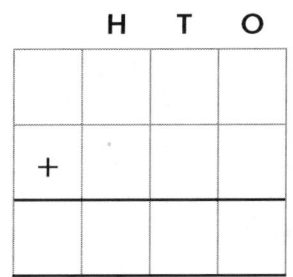
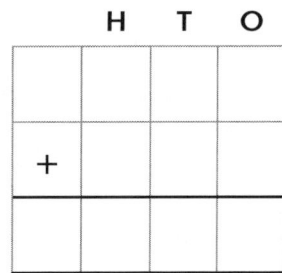
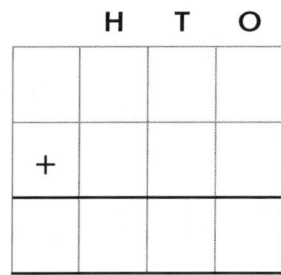
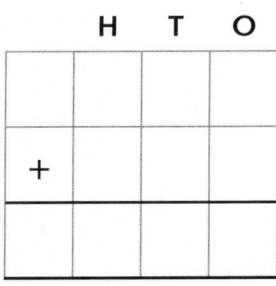
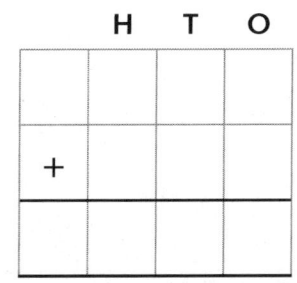

Name: _____ Date: _____

Add numbers mentally

Add numbers mentally and use the inverse operation to check the answer

1 Add multiples of 10. Draw a number line if you need to.

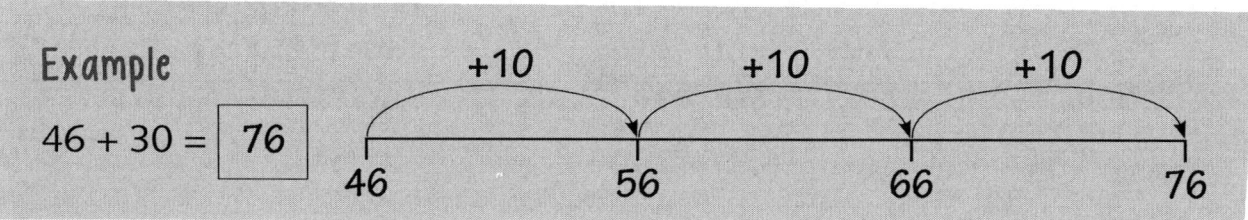

Example

46 + 30 = 76

a 34 + 30 = ☐

b 28 + 40 = ☐

c 37 + 40 = ☐

d 41 + 30 = ☐

e 45 + 50 = ☐

Working out

2 Add multiples of 100. Draw a number line if you need to.

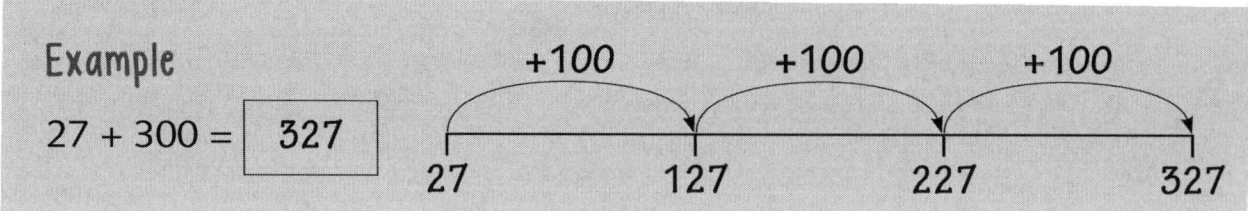

Example

27 + 300 = 327

a 36 + 200 = ☐

b 48 + 300 = ☐

c 71 + 400 = ☐

d 62 + 300 = ☐

e 85 + 500 = ☐

Working out

Name: _____ Date: _____

ubtracting Is and 10s

Subtract 2-digit numbers using the formal written method
of column subtraction

Subtract these 2-digit numbers using the
formal written method of column subtraction.
Practising with two-digit numbers
will help you learn the method.

Example		T	O
54 – 21 =		5	4
	–	2	1
		3	3

1 86 – 42 =

2 68 – 35 =

3 49 – 26 =

4 57 – 32 =

5 74 – 51 =

6 86 – 43 =

7 67 – 25 =

8 76 – 34 =

9 83 – 41 =

10 95 – 31 =

11 73 – 22 =

12 89 – 33 =

Name: _____ Date: _____

Subtraction instructions

Subtract 3-digit numbers using the formal
written method of column subtraction

1 Write a set of instructions for using the column method of subtraction.

   When you have written your instructions, ask a partner to use them.

   _____
   _____
   _____
   _____
   _____
   _____
   _____
   _____
   _____
   _____
   _____

2 The letters a, b and c below all represent a different digit.

   • a is less than b.

   • a is not 0 (zero).

$$\begin{array}{r} b\ a \\ -\ a\ b \\ \hline c\ 6 \end{array}$$

What could the digits be? There are five different possible answers.

[ ] [ ] [ ]   [ ] [ ] [ ]   [ ] [ ] [ ]

[ ] [ ] [ ]   [ ] [ ] [ ]

Name: _____ Date: _____

Subtracting 10s and 100s

Subtract numbers mentally and use the inverse operation to check the answer

1 Subtract multiples of 10. Draw a number line if you need to.

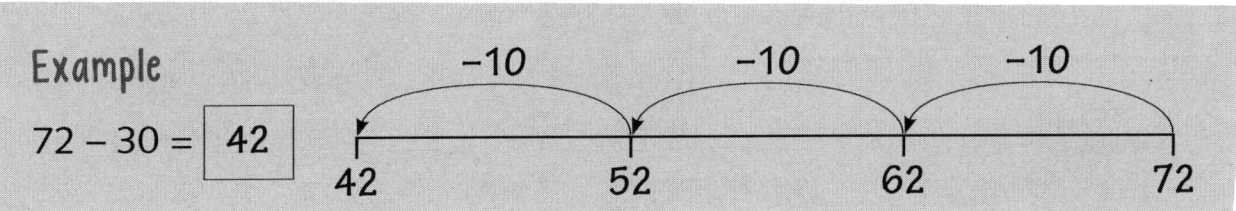

Example

$72 - 30 =$ 42

−10   −10   −10

42   52   62   72

a $74 - 30 =$ ☐

b $62 - 40 =$ ☐

c $81 - 30 =$ ☐

d $75 - 40 =$ ☐

e $67 - 20 =$ ☐

Working out

2 Subtract multiples of 100. Draw a number line if you need to.

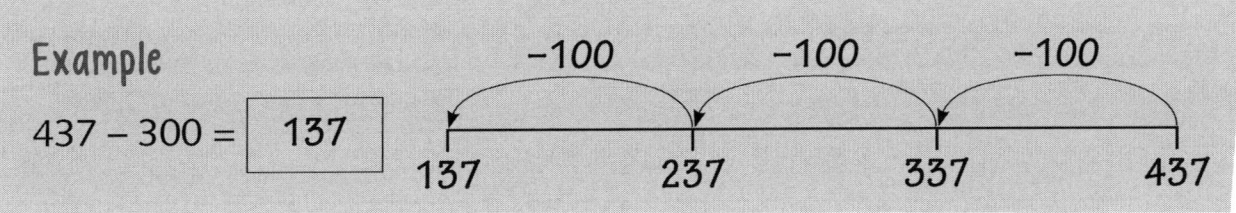

Example

$437 - 300 =$ 137

−100   −100   −100

137   237   337   437

a $428 - 200 =$ ☐

b $381 - 200 =$ ☐

c $457 - 300 =$ ☐

d $528 - 400 =$ ☐

e $485 - 400 =$ ☐

Working out

Name: _____ Date: _____

Sports problems

- Add and subtract amounts of money
- Solve problems involving money and reason mathematically

School Sports Equipment

£600

£572

£236

£200

£155

Make up your own problems about buying equipment from the sports shop. Add two of your own items.

You must work out your problems so you know the answers!

1 _____

_____

2 _____

_____

3 _____

_____

4 _____

_____

5 _____

_____

6 _____

_____

Name: _____ Date: _____

Fruit and vegetable charts

Interpret and present data using tables and charts

1 Make a tally mark in the table for each item.

Item	Tally
apples	|||
bananas	
carrots	
mushrooms	
pears	

2 Count the tally marks and complete the frequency table.

Item	Frequency
apples	3
bananas	
carrots	
mushrooms	
pears	

3 How many more bananas are there than:

　　a apples? ☐　　**b** pears? ☐

4 a The total number of fruits is ☐.

　　b The total number of vegetables is ☐.

　　c There are ☐ fewer fruits than vegetables.

Name: _____ Date: _____

Counters pictogram

Interpret and present data in pictograms where one picture represents 2 units

You will need:
• bag containing about 40 counters or centicubes in three colours

1 Play this game with a partner.

- Take turns to:
  - take a counter from the bag
  - make a tally mark in the table for the colour of your counter.

- Continue until the bag is empty.

Colour of counter	Tally	Frequency

- Write the frequency for each colour.

2 Use the data in the table above and complete the pictogram below.

Counters

Number of counters   Key: ◯ = 2 counters

3 The most common colour of counter

is _____.

The least common colour of counter

is _____.

Name: _____ Date: _____

Dice pictograms

Show data in a pictogram where
a picture represents 2 units

1 Decide who is Player A and who is Player B.

  • Take turns to:
    – roll the dice
    – colour a square in the grid of your score card for your score.

The winner is the first player to complete any row of six squares.

Player A score card

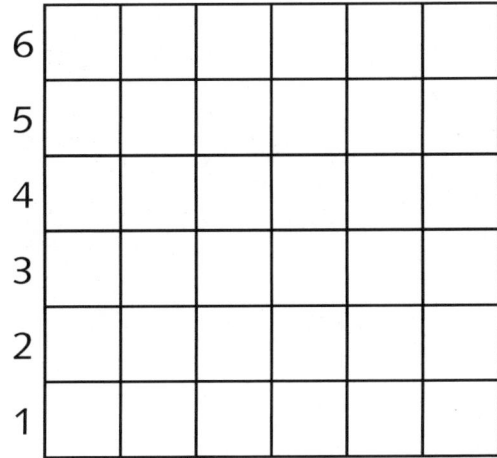

Player B score card

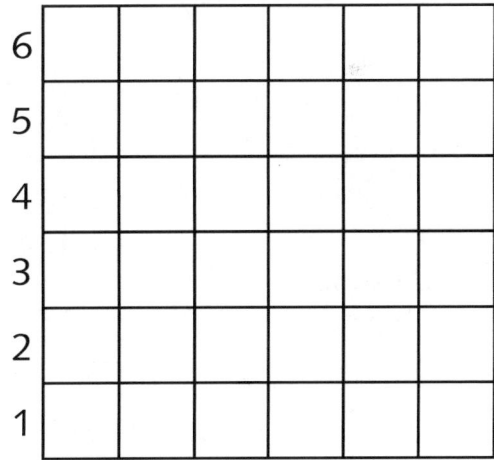

2 Complete the table with the scores for both players.

	1	2	3	4	5	6
Player A						
Player B						
Total						

3 Use the totals in the table and complete the pictogram.

Dice game

6					
5					
4					
3					
2					
1					

Number of rolls of the dice

Key: ■ = 2 rolls of dice

Name: _____ Date: _____

Capacity bar chart

Show data in a bar chart with intervals labelled in 2s

1 Look at the capacities shown on these containers.

Complete the bar chart.

carton of
apple juice
1 litre

bottle
of cola
500 ml

bottle of
shampoo
400 ml

jar of salad
dressing
200 ml

bottle of
tomato sauce
100 ml

Container capacities

Capacity in millilitres

1000
800
600
400
200
0

apple   cola   salad   tomato shampoo
juice   dressing sauce

Contents

2 Which container holds:

a the least amount? _____

b the greatest amount? _____

3 What is the middle-sized container filled with? _____

4 Which container holds twice as much as:

a the bottle of cola? _____

b the jar of salad dressing? _____

5 How many bottles of tomato sauce have the same capacity
as the container of?

a shampoo? ☐

b apple juice? ☐

Name: _____ Date: _____

evising multiplication facts

Consolidate recall of the multiplication facts for
the 2, 3, 4, 5, 8 and 10 multiplication tables

Play this game with a partner.

You will need:
• 20 counters

What to do:

• Cover each number fact with a counter.

• Take turns to:
  – remove a counter
  – say the answer to the multiplication fact.

• Check the answer with your partner.

• If you are correct, keep the counter.
  If you are incorrect, place the counter
  back on the board.

• Continue until all the counters have been removed.

• The player with the most counters at the end is the winner.

3 × 3	8 × 12	7 × 3	11 × 10
5 × 8	8 × 3	8 × 4	9 × 5
12 × 5	9 × 8	4 × 4	6 × 4
9 × 4	6 × 8	3 × 8	8 × 2
8 × 8	8 × 7	5 × 4	6 × 3

Name: _____ Date: _____

Revising multiplication facts

Consolidate recall of the multiplication facts for the 2, 3, 4, 5, 8 and 10 multiplication tables, and related facts involving multiples of 10

Complete each table.

1

×	5	4	3
3			
6		24	
9			
12			

2

×	2	3	5	10	12
2					
4					
6					72
8					
10					

3

×	2	3	4	5	8	10
7						
3				15		
9						
4						
11						

4

×	2	4	8
	12		
		36	
			56
30			
50			
	160		

5

×		3	8	10	4
				80	
4	20				
		90			
50					
80					

Name: _____ **Date:** _____

Revising division facts

Recall the division facts for the 2, 3, 4, 5, 8 and 10 multiplication tables

Play this game with a partner.

What to do:

You will need:
- 20 counters

- Cover each number fact with a counter.
- Take turns to:
    - remove a counter
    - say the answer to the division fact.

- Check the answer with your partner.
- If you are correct, keep the counter.
  If you are incorrect, place the counter
  back on the board.
- Continue until all the counters have been removed.
- The player with the most counters at the end is the winner.

40 ÷ 8	64 ÷ 8	32 ÷ 8	21 ÷ 3	18 ÷ 3
9 ÷ 3	48 ÷ 8	27 ÷ 3	45 ÷ 5	20 ÷ 4
100 ÷ 10	16 ÷ 2	96 ÷ 8	72 ÷ 8	15 ÷ 3
60 ÷ 5	28 ÷ 4	36 ÷ 4	24 ÷ 8	56 ÷ 8

Name: _____ Date: _____

Solving problems

Solve problems and reason mathematically

Answer these word problems. Show all your working.

1 There are 36 pencils in a box. How many pencils are there in 3 boxes?

☐

2 There are 5 flowers in a vase. How many flowers are there in 12 vases?

☐

3 Motorbikes have 2 wheels. How many wheels do 90 motorbikes have?

☐

4 A jar holds 56 biscuits. 8 biscuits are eaten. How many are left?

☐

5 Tricycles have 3 wheels. How many wheels are there altogether if there are 60 tricycles?

☐

6 A train has 6 carriages. Each carriage has 20 rows of seats and each row has 4 seats. How many seats are there altogether on the train?

☐

7 Plants are arranged so that there are 8 in each row. How many plants are there 9 rows?

☐

8 There are 35 biscuits and 5 children. How many biscuits can each child have?

☐

9 Sweets are red, blue, green, yellow, pink, orange, purple and brown in colour. If there are 40 of each colour, how many sweets are there altogether?

☐

10 If there are 240 legs, how many octopuses are there?

☐

Name: _____ Date: _____

Pizza problem

Compare and order unit fractions, and fractions with the same denominator

 pepperoni   mushroom  tuna   pineapple

1 Choose three different toppings.

Using pizzas that are divided into sixths, how many pizzas can you create?

You can only use one topping per slice.

a   b   c   d

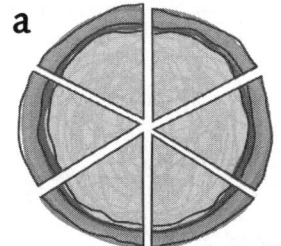 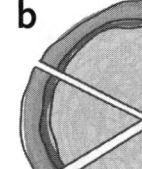  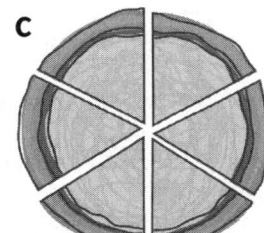 

e   f   g

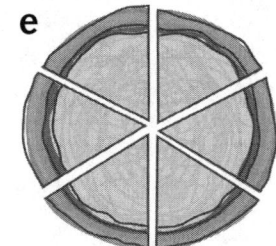 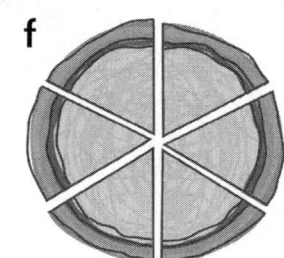 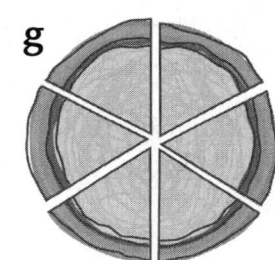

2 Write a fraction addition calculation for each pizza.

Example 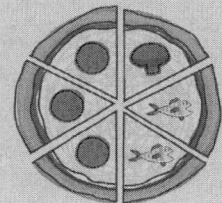 $\frac{1}{6} + \frac{2}{6} + \frac{3}{6}$

a $\dfrac{\square}{\square} + \dfrac{\square}{\square} + \dfrac{\square}{\square}$

b $\dfrac{\square}{\square} + \dfrac{\square}{\square} + \dfrac{\square}{\square}$ c $\dfrac{\square}{\square} + \dfrac{\square}{\square} + \dfrac{\square}{\square}$ d $\dfrac{\square}{\square} + \dfrac{\square}{\square} + \dfrac{\square}{\square}$

e $\dfrac{\square}{\square} + \dfrac{\square}{\square} + \dfrac{\square}{\square}$ f $\dfrac{\square}{\square} + \dfrac{\square}{\square} + \dfrac{\square}{\square}$ g $\dfrac{\square}{\square} + \dfrac{\square}{\square} + \dfrac{\square}{\square}$

Name: _____ Date: _____

Subtracting snakes

Subtract fractions within 1 whole

1 Use the snakes to help you subtract the fractions.

a $\frac{3}{3} - \frac{1}{3} =$ ☐   I am a $\frac{3}{3}$ snake.

b $\frac{5}{5} - \frac{2}{5} =$ ☐   I am a $\frac{5}{5}$ snake.

2 Now cross out parts yourself and then subtract the fractions.

a $\frac{5}{5} - \frac{4}{5} =$ ☐   I am a $\frac{5}{5}$ snake.

b $\frac{6}{6} - \frac{1}{6} =$ ☐   I am a $\frac{6}{6}$ snake.

c $\frac{6}{6} - \frac{4}{6} =$ ☐   I am a $\frac{6}{6}$ snake.

d $\frac{8}{8} - \frac{3}{8} =$ ☐   I am a $\frac{8}{8}$ snake.

e $\frac{8}{8} - \frac{6}{8} =$ ☐   I am a $\frac{8}{8}$ snake.

f $\frac{10}{10} - \frac{2}{10} =$ ☐   I am a $\frac{10}{10}$ snake.

3 Draw your own snake and write a subtraction calculation to go with it.

Name: _____ Date: _____

Subtracting beyond I whole

Subtract fractions beyond one whole

Use the diagrams to answer the fraction subtraction calculations.

1 $1\frac{2}{5} - \frac{4}{5} =$ ☐

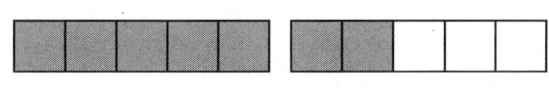

2 $1\frac{1}{6} - \frac{3}{6} =$ ☐

3 $1\frac{4}{7} - \frac{6}{7} =$ ☐

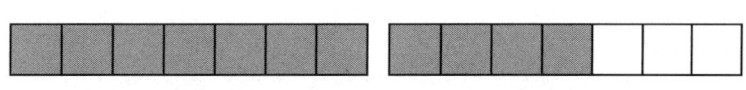

4 $1\frac{3}{8} - \frac{7}{8} =$ ☐

5 $1\frac{5}{8} - \frac{8}{8} =$ ☐

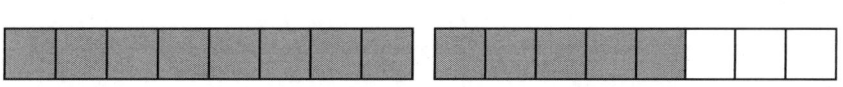

6 $1\frac{3}{9} - \frac{6}{9} =$ ☐

7 $2\frac{1}{2} - 1\frac{1}{2} =$ ☐

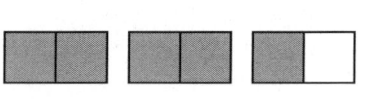

8 $2\frac{1}{4} - \frac{3}{4} =$ ☐

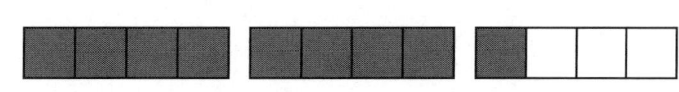

Name: _____ Date: _____

Building fractions

Recognise equivalent fractions

You will need:
• coloured pencils

1 Write the fractions on to the fraction wall.

   a Shade in two-quarters.

   b Shade in three-sixths.

   c Shade in four-eighths.

   d Shade in five-tenths.

2 What do you notice about all of these fractions?

_____

_____

Name: _____ Date: _____

erimeters of rectangles

Calculate the perimeter of rectangles in centimetres

Two sides of a rectangle have been drawn.
Complete each rectangle.
Find its perimeter in centimetres.

Example

perimeter = | 14 | cm

1

perimeter = [   ] cm

2

perimeter = [   ] cm

3

perimeter = [   ] cm

4

perimeter = [   ] cm

5

perimeter = [   ] cm

6

perimeter = [   ] cm

7

perimeter = [   ] cm

8

perimeter = [   ] cm

9

perimeter = [   ] cm

10

perimeter
= [   ] cm

Name: _____ Date: _____

Predicting perimeters

Using a ruler, draw and calculate
the perimeter of rectangles

You will need:
• ruler

1 Draw the next three rectangles in the pattern.

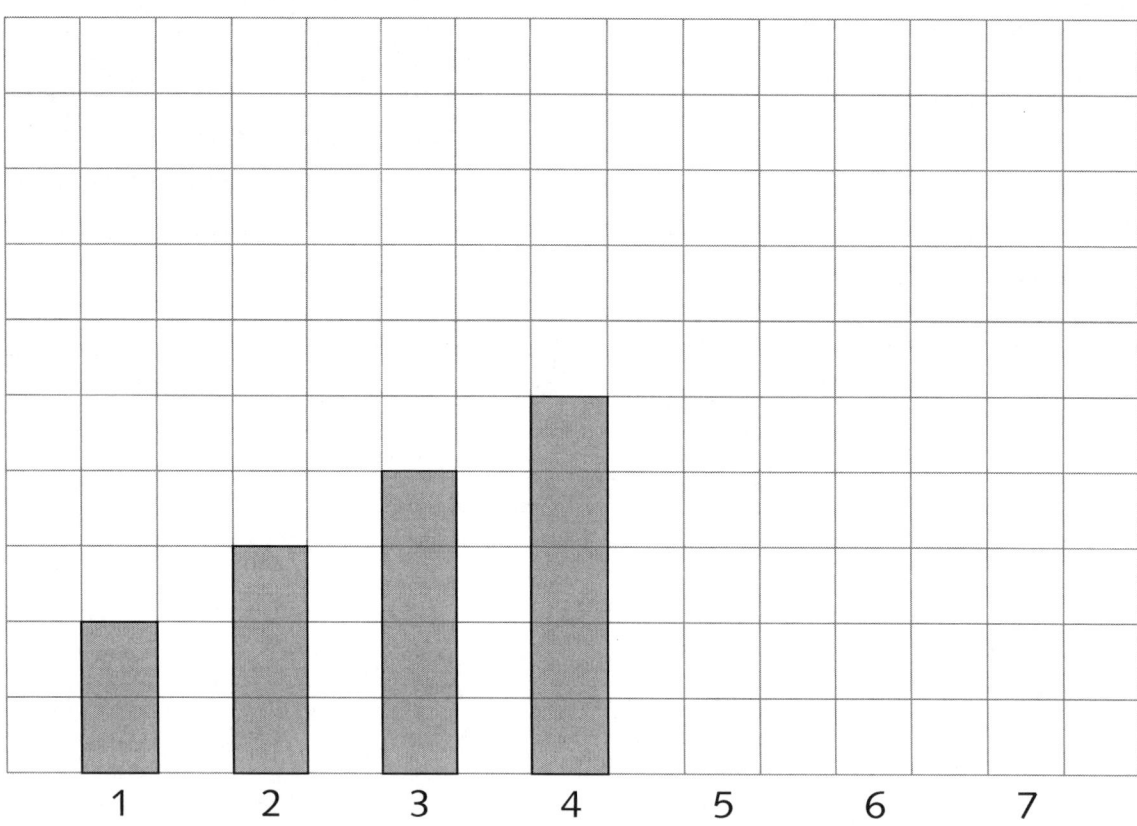

2 Complete the table.

Rectangle	1	2	3	4	5	6	7
Perimeter	cm	cm	cm	cm	cm	cm	cm

3 Write about the pattern you notice.

_____

_____

4 Use the pattern to predict the perimeter of:

a Rectangle 10 [ ] cm   **b** Rectangle 12 [ ] cm

Name: _____ Date: _____

erimeter patterns

Measure and calculate the
perimeter of regular 2-D shapes

You will need:
• ruler

Work out the perimeter of each shape and write it in the centre of the shape.

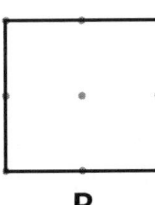
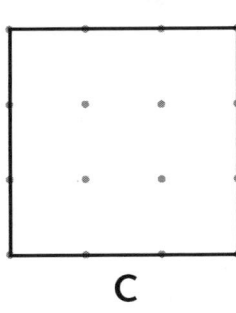
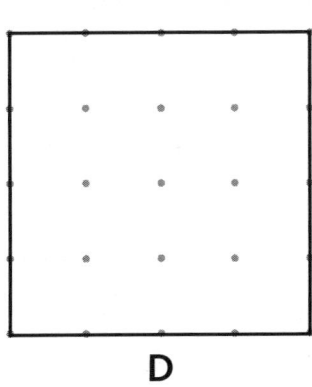

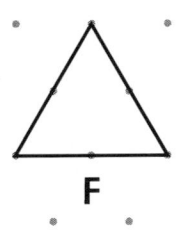
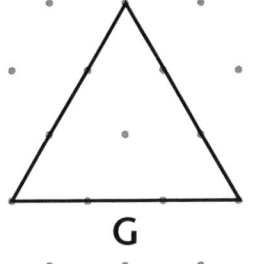
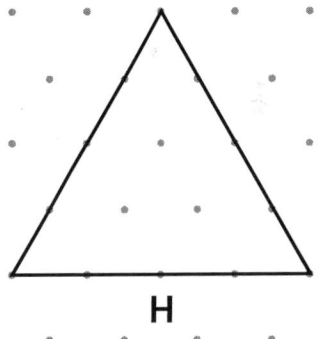

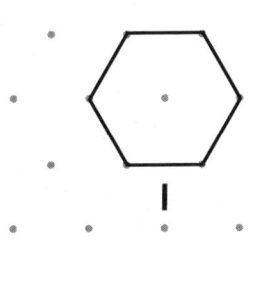
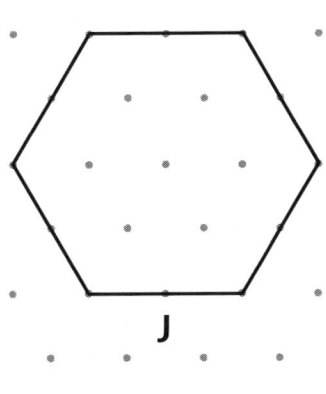
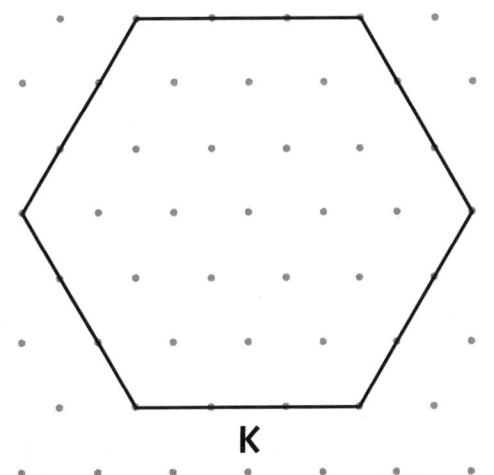

Name: _____ Date: _____

Hexagonal hunt

Measure and calculate the
perimeter of 2-D shapes

You will need:
• ruler
• triangular dot paper

1 The dots on the grid are 1 cm apart.

Each shape is made by joining four hexagons.

Find the perimeter of these shapes in centimetres.

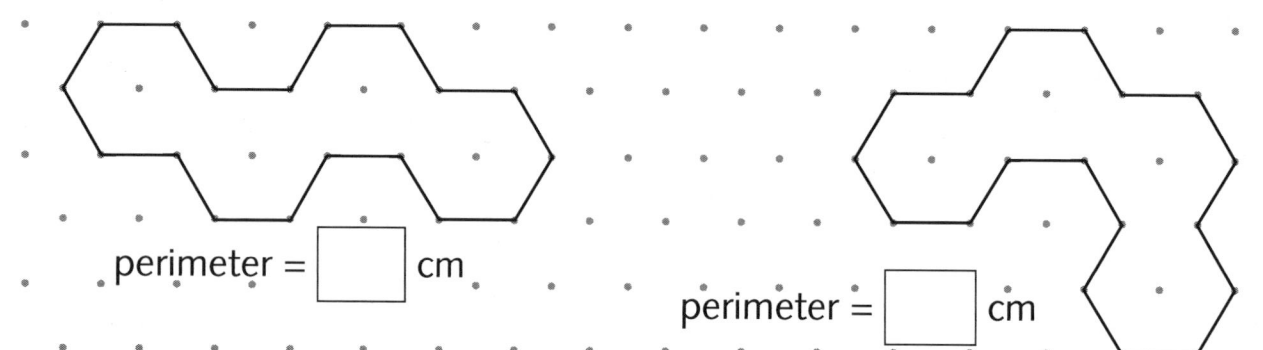

perimeter = ⬚ cm

perimeter = ⬚ cm

2 Draw different shapes made by joining four hexagons. Work out the
perimeter of each of your shapes.

3 What if you fitted together five hexagons? How many different shapes
could you draw? Use the triangular dot paper to find out.

Name: _____ Date: _____

Digit sum tickets

Order numbers to 1000

1 Lucky Laura chooses her raffle tickets carefully.
She only buys tickets if the digits add up to eight.

521

I can buy this ticket as $5 + 2 + 1 = 8$.

What are some of the tickets she could buy?

2 Order the numbers you have made, smallest to largest.

smallest

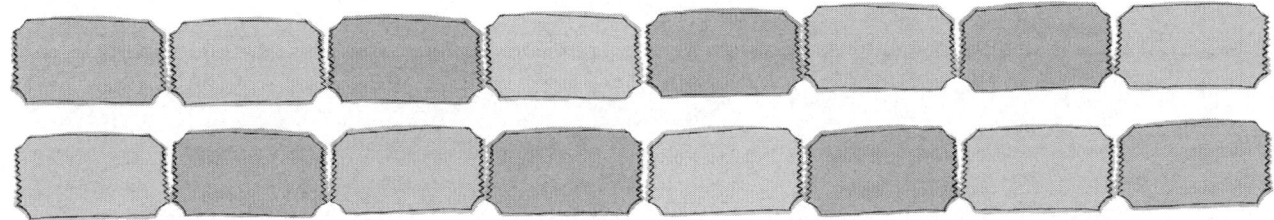

largest

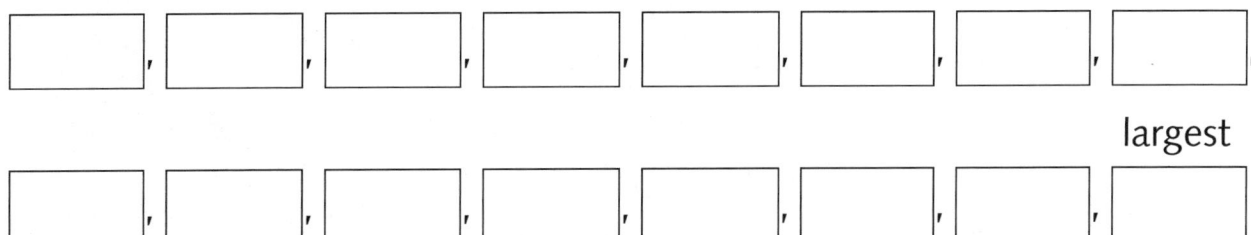

3 Now Laura has decided she only wants even numbers.

Circle the tickets she can still buy.

4 Do you think even numbers are more likely to be picked out of the raffle?
Explain why.

_____

_____

Name: _____ Date: _____

On the number line

Order 2-digit numbers

1 Put these numbers in the correct place on the number line.

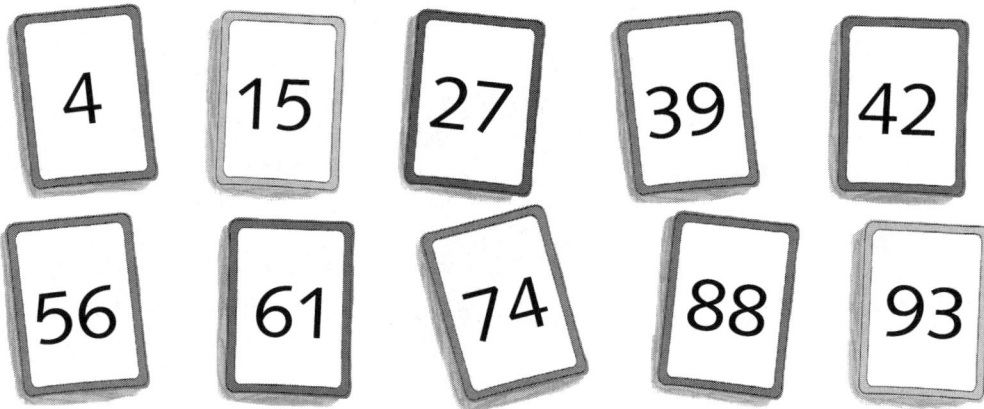

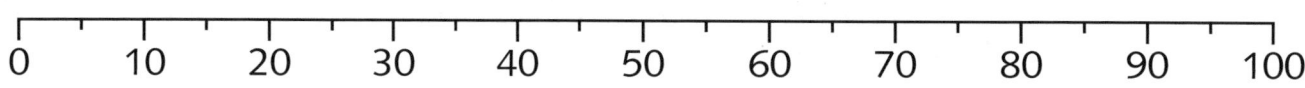

2 Now think of your own 2-digit numbers. Write them here.

3 Write them in the correct place on the number line.

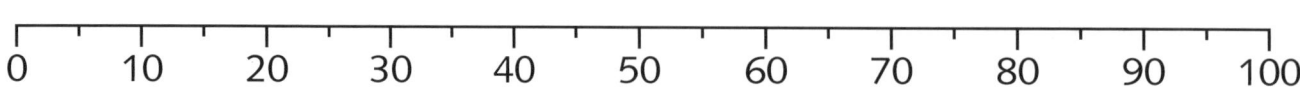

4 Swap with a partner and check each other's number lines.

Name: _____ Date: _____

Find my number

Partition 3-digit numbers in various ways

1 Hannah has thought of a 3-digit number.

Here is her clue.

$\boxed{}00 + 320 + 41 = ?$

What might her number be?

2 George has thought of a number.

Here is his clue.

$200 + \boxed{} + 35 = ?$

What might his number be?

3 Explain why there are more possible answers for George's number than Hannah's.

_____

_____

4 Make up a secret 3-digit number for a friend. Write your clue here.

$\boxed{} + \boxed{} + \boxed{} = ?$

Name: _____ Date: _____

Circle the numbers

Solve number problems and
reason mathematically

1	2	3	4	5	6	7	8	9	10
11	12	13	14	15	16	17	18	19	20
21	22	23	24	25	26	27	28	29	30
31	32	33	34	35	36	37	38	39	40
41	42	43	44	45	46	47	48	49	50
51	52	53	54	55	56	57	58	59	60
61	62	63	64	65	66	67	68	69	70
71	72	73	74	75	76	77	78	79	80
81	82	83	84	85	86	87	88	89	90
91	92	93	94	95	96	97	98	99	100

Work with a partner.

1 a Circle six numbers
on the 100 square.

b Complete the table.
One line has been done for you.

My number	One more	One less	A larger number	A smaller number	Odd or even?	10s	1s
35	36	34	73	26	Odd	30	5

2 Find this secret number.

a It is between 50 and 60.   **b** It is even.   **c** The 1s digit is higher than 4.

The number is ⬜ or ⬜ .

3 Now choose your own secret number. Write it here ⬜ .

Write three things about it.

a It is _____.

b It is _____.

c The 1s digit is _____.

Name: _____ Date: _____

Mental addition and subtraction

Add and subtract numbers mentally

1 Use the number lines to add the multiples of 10 and 100.

a 267 + 60

267 ⌐—————————————————————————¬

b 158 + 300

158 ⌐—————————————————————————¬

c 249 + 500

249 ⌐—————————————————————————¬

d 271 + 50

271 ⌐—————————————————————————¬

e 373 + 30

373 ⌐—————————————————————————¬

f 382 + 400

382 ⌐—————————————————————————¬

2 Use the number lines to subtract the multiples of 10 and 100.

a 286 − 40

⌐—————————————————————————¬ 286

b 251 − 70

⌐—————————————————————————¬ 251

c 528 − 300

⌐—————————————————————————¬ 528

d 456 − 60

⌐—————————————————————————¬ 456

e 615 − 400

⌐—————————————————————————¬ 615

f 759 − 700

⌐—————————————————————————¬ 759

Name: _____ Date: _____

Challenge your partner (l)

- Add 3-digit numbers using the formal written method of column addition
- Estimate and check the answer to a calculation

Work with a partner.

1 Write a 3-digit number in the first box of all the calculations in the calculation column below. Then swap papers with your partner.

2 Fill in the second numbers of all the calculations on your partner's sheet.

3 Take your sheet back and work out the answers to the calculations.

4 Swap back and check each other's work.

Calculation	Working out	Checking
☐ + ☐ = ☐		
☐ + ☐ = ☐		
☐ + ☐ = ☐		
☐ + ☐ = ☐		
☐ + ☐ = ☐		
☐ + ☐ = ☐		

Name: _____ Date: _____

Challenge your partner (2)

- Subtract 3-digit numbers using the formal written method of column subtraction
- Estimate and check the answer to a calculation

Work with a partner.

1 Write a 3-digit number greater than 500 in the first box of all the calculations below. Then swap papers with your partner.

2 Fill in the second numbers of all the calculations on your partner's sheet. Make sure the second number is smaller than the first.

3 Take your sheet back and work out the answers to the calculations.

4 Swap back and check each other's work.

Calculation	Working out	Checking
☐ – ☐ = ☐		
☐ – ☐ = ☐		
☐ – ☐ = ☐		
☐ – ☐ = ☐		
☐ – ☐ = ☐		
☐ – ☐ = ☐		

Name: _____ Date: _____

Word problems

Solve problems and reason mathematically

Work out the answer to each problem.

Addition facts

7 eggs were dropped and broken on Monday and 9 eggs on Tuesday. How many eggs altogether were broken?

Working out:

Subtraction facts

Year 2 collected 16 eggs and used 7 to make an omelette. How many were left?

Working out:

Mental addition

The café bought 78 eggs one week, and then ordered 60 more. How many eggs did they need altogether?

Mental subtraction

At the beginning of the year, 450 kg of food was ordered. So far the chickens have eaten 200 g. How much food is left?

Column addition

One half term 261 eggs were collected, and 227 the next half term. How many eggs altogether?

Working out:

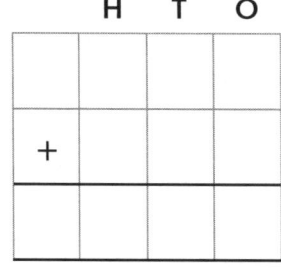

Column subtraction

One half term 275 eggs were collected, 142 of them were sold. How many eggs were left for the school?

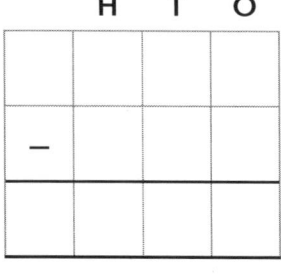

Working out:

Name: _____ Date: _____

rawing spirals

Know when a line is horizontal or vertical

1 This spiral was made with horizontal and vertical lines.

a Continue the spiral as far as you can go.

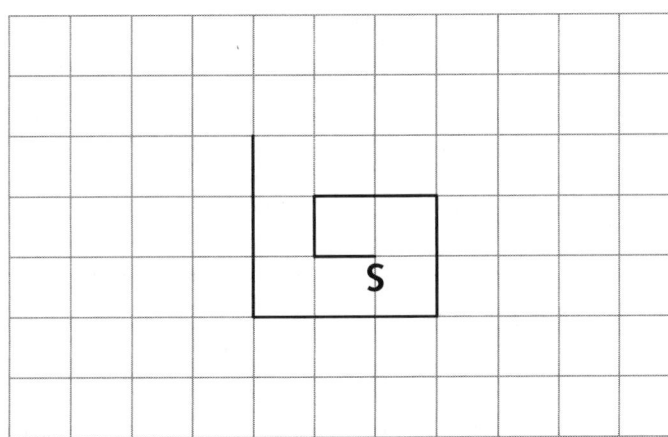

b Highlight the horizontal lines blue and the vertical lines red.

c Complete the route for your spiral.

S, 1H, 1V, 2H, 2V, _____

2 Draw and then highlight this spiral on the squared grid below.

S, 10H, 9V, 8H, 7V, 6H, 5V, 4H, 3V, 2H, 1V.

H = horizontal
V = vertical

Hint
Think carefully before you begin about where on the grid to start.

Name: _____ Date: _____

Pairs of lines

Recognise perpendicular and parallel lines

You will need:
• ruler
• set square or
  right-angle tester

1 For each line below draw a second line that is **parallel** to it.

a   b   c   d

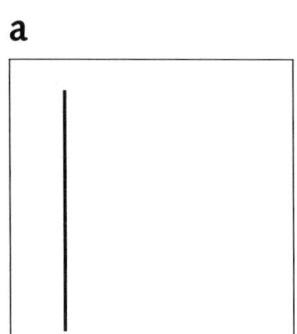 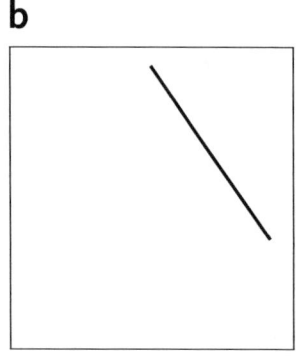  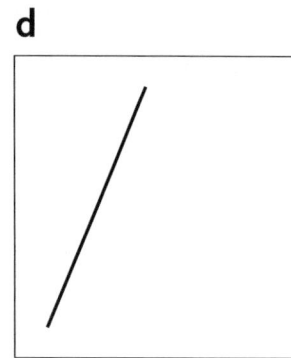

2 For each line below draw a second line that is **perpendicular** (at right angles) to it.

a   b   c   d

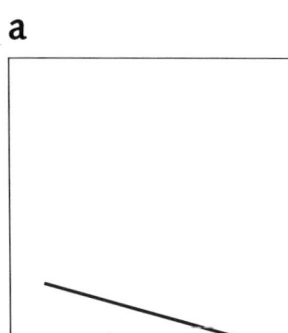 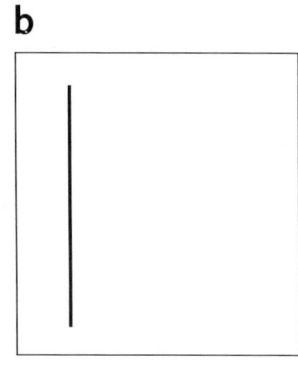 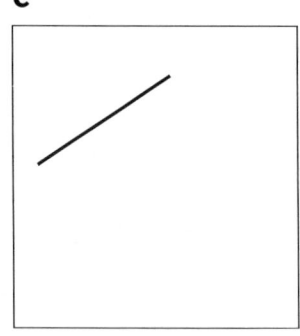 

3 For each line below draw a second line that is neither **parallel** nor **perpendicular** (at right angles) to it.

a   b   c   d

 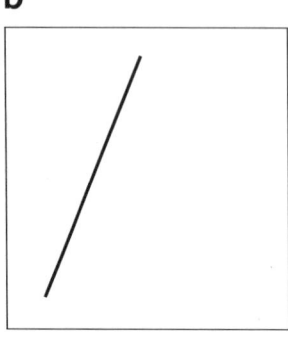 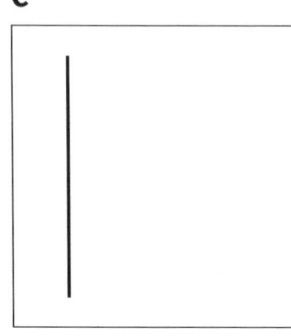 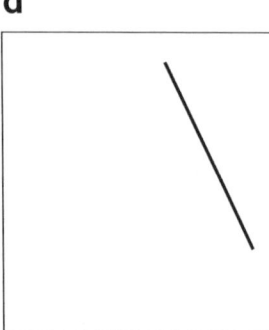

Name: _____ Date: _____

Lines on a 9-dot grid

Recognise perpendicular and parallel lines

You will need:
• ruler
• red pencil

1 In grids 1 to 20 find as many different ways to draw two parallel lines as you can.

The lines must be straight, between two dots, without crossing a dot.

2 In each grid draw, in red, a perpendicular line which joins the two parallel lines.

1

2

3

4

5

6

7

8

9

10

11

12

13

14

15

16

17

18

19

20

Name: _____ Date: _____

Shape shopping list

Describe the properties of 2-D shapes

You will need:
- right-angle tester
- coloured pencil

1 Draw a line to join each shape to its description.

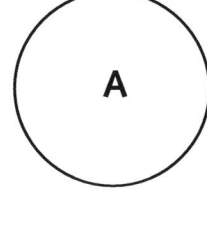

A

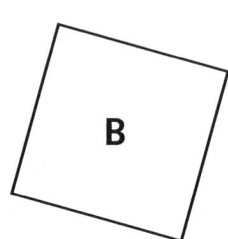

B

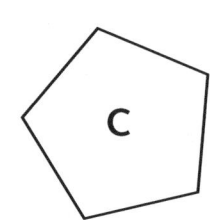

C

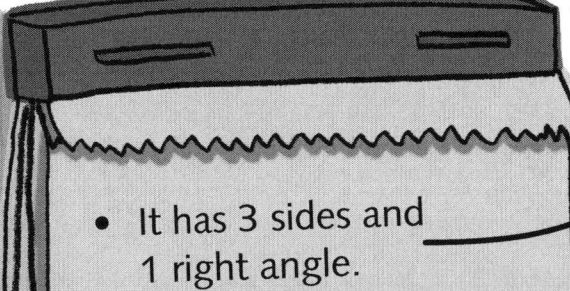

E

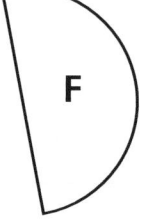

F

- It has 3 sides and 1 right angle.
- Its 4 sides are all different lengths.
- It is half of a circle.
- Its only edge is curved.
- It has 6 vertices and no right angles.
- It has 4 sides and 1 right angle.
- It has 5 equal sides.
- All the sides and angles are equal.

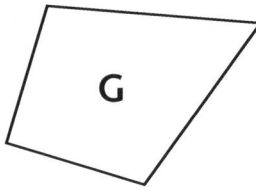

G

D

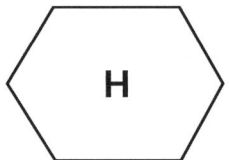

H

2 Write the letters of the shapes in the table.

All right angles	Some right angles	No right angles
	E,	

Name: _____ Date: _____

Multiplication using partitioning

Use partitioning to calculate TO × O

Estimate the answer first then partition each of these calculations to work out the answer.

Example

$63 \times 5 \rightarrow$ ($60 \times 5 = 300$)

$= (60 \times 5) + (3 \times 5)$
$= 300 + 15$
$= 315$

1 $45 \times 3 \rightarrow$

=

=

=

2 $52 \times 4 \rightarrow$

=

=

=

3 $34 \times 5 \rightarrow$

=

=

=

4 $29 \times 3 \rightarrow$

=

=

=

5 $58 \times 2 \rightarrow$

=

=

=

6 $64 \times 4 \rightarrow$

=

=

=

7 $39 \times 5 \rightarrow$

=

=

=

Name: _____ Date: _____

Multiplication using partitioning and the grid method

Use the grid method to calculate TO × O

Estimate the answer first then use the grid method to work out the answer.

Example

43 × 5 → (40 × 5 = 200)

×	40	3	
5	200	15	= 215

1 64 × 2 →

2 43 × 3 →
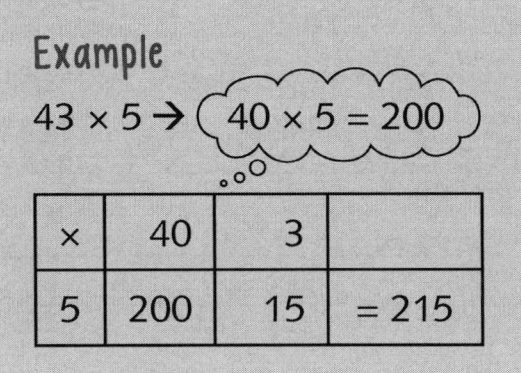

3 39 × 4 →
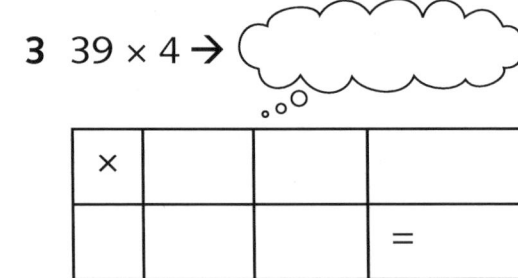

4 65 × 5 →
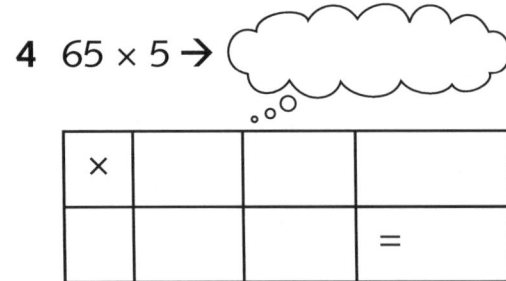

5 48 × 4 →
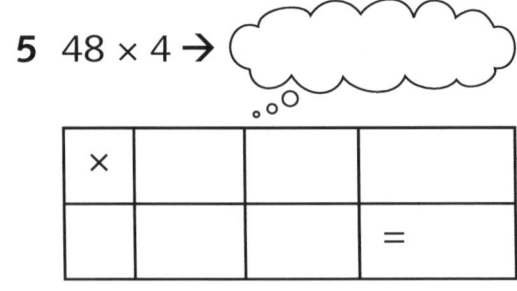

6 57 × 3 →
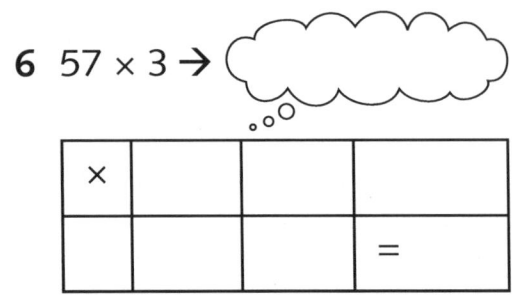

7 23 × 8 →
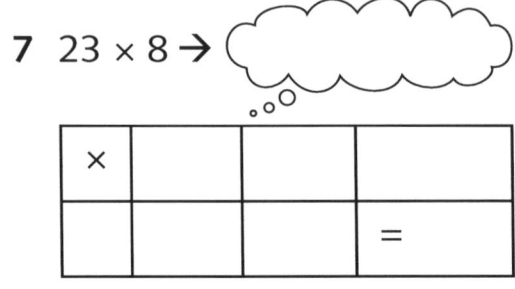

Name: _____ Date: _____

Multiplication: Introducing the expanded written method

Use the expanded written method to calculate TO × O

Estimate the answer first then use the grid method to work out the answer.

Example

63 × 8 → (60 × 8 = 480)

H	T	O	
	6	3	
×		8	
	2	4	(3 × 8)
4	8	0	(60 × 8)
5	0	4	
1			

1 87 × 4 →

H   T   O

H	T	O	
×			

2 79 × 3 →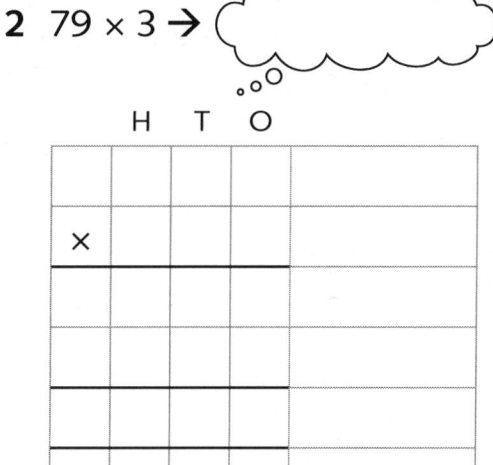

H   T   O

H	T	O	
×			

3 48 × 5 →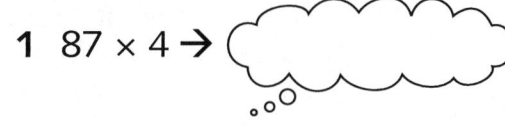

H   T   O

H	T	O	
×			

4 94 × 8 →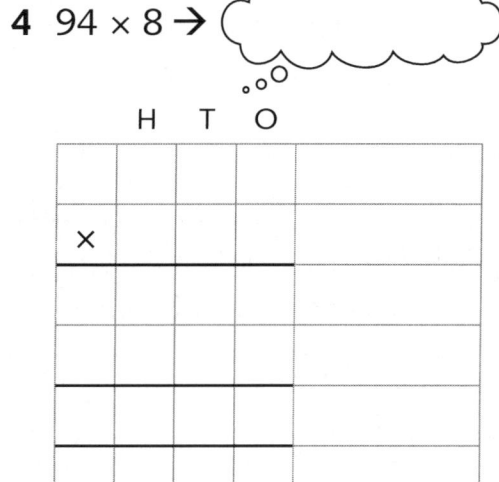

H   T   O

H	T	O	
×			

Name: _____ Date: _____

Solving problems

Solve problems and reason mathematically

Calculate the answer to these problems.

76 apples

48 oranges

64 lemons

56 pears

39 mangoes

83 strawberries

1 Buy 8 boxes of pears and 2 boxes of lemons. How many pieces of fruit altogether?	**2** Boxes of oranges are split into bags of 4 oranges per bag. How many bags of oranges can be made?
3 Buy 3 boxes of strawberries. Eat 35. How many strawberries left?	**4** Buy 8 boxes of mangoes and 8 boxes of apples. How many pieces of fruit altogether?
5 Mangoes cost £2 each. How much does it cost for 4 boxes of mangoes?	**6** Buy one box of each fruit. How many pieces of fruit altogether?
7 Buy 3 boxes of pears and 4 boxes of apples. How many more apples than pears are there?	**8** Buy 3 boxes of apples. Buy 4 boxes of pears. Which fruit do you have more of?

Name: _____ Date: _____

inding fractions

Find fractions of amounts

You will need:
• 12 counters

Take 12 counters.

Use the boxes below to see if they can be divided into these fractions.

Put a ✓ or ✗ next to the fractions.

Fraction	✓ or ✗
Halves	
Thirds	
Quarters	
Sixths	

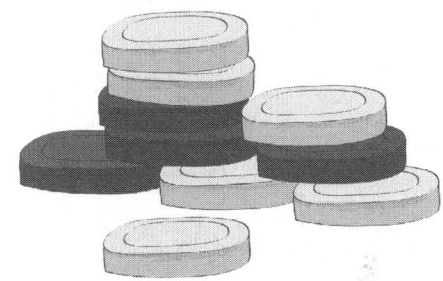

Remember fractions are always equal so you must have the same amount in each box.

- Halves $\frac{1}{2}$

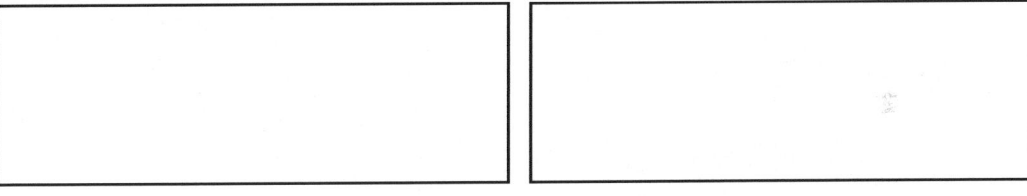

- Thirds $\frac{1}{3}$

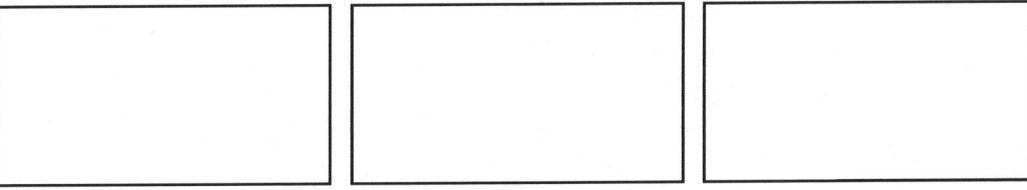

- Quarters $\frac{1}{4}$

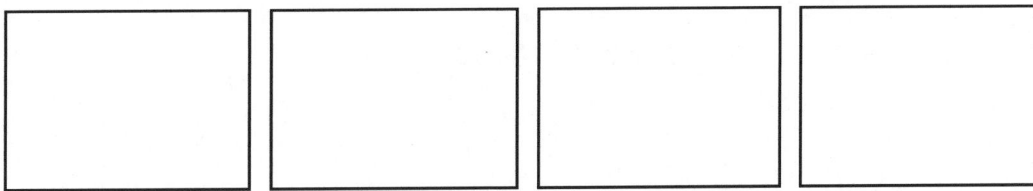

- Sixths $\frac{1}{6}$

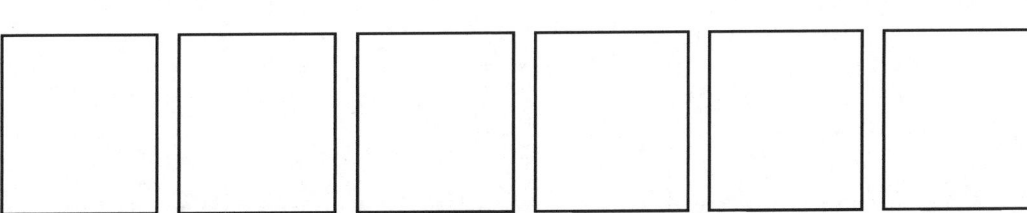

Name: _____ Date: _____

Pound fractions

Find fractions of amounts

1 What does Hannah spend her money on?

Show your working out in the box.

Hannah has £1.

She spends half at the sweet shop.

She spends a quarter on an apple.

She loses a tenth.

How much is left?

2 What does Connor spend his money on?

Show your working out in the box.

Connor has £1.20.

He spends a quarter on an orange.

He spends a third on a carton of juice.

He spends a sixth on a chocolate bar.

How much is left?

3 Make up your own fraction money question for a friend to work out.

Make sure you know the answer!

_____

_____

_____

_____

_____

Name: _____ Date: _____

equivalent patterns

Recognise equivalent fractions

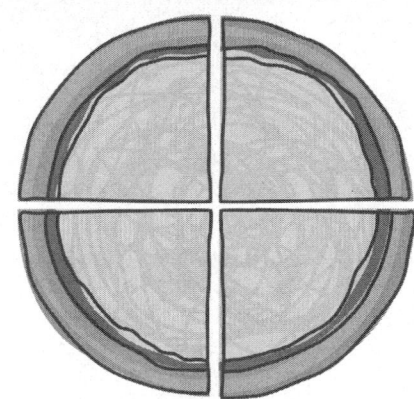

1 Draw a diagram or picture to show that these fractions are equivalent.

a $\frac{1}{2} = \frac{2}{4} = \frac{3}{6}$

b $\frac{1}{3} = \frac{2}{6} = \frac{3}{9}$

2 What do you notice about the numerators and denominators?

_____

_____

_____

Name: _____ Date: _____

Tenths on number lines

Count up and down in tenths

You will need:
• coloured
  pencil

1 Colour in the tenths on each of these number tracks.

Example

$\frac{3}{10}$ [■■■□□□□□□□]

a $\frac{5}{10}$

b $\frac{2}{10}$

c $\frac{6}{10}$

d $\frac{8}{10}$

e $\frac{4}{10}$

f $\frac{9}{10}$

2 Fill in the missing tenths on these number tracks.

a

$\frac{1}{10}$	$\frac{2}{10}$		$\frac{4}{10}$		$\frac{6}{10}$	$\frac{7}{10}$			1

b

	$\frac{2}{10}$	$\frac{3}{10}$		$\frac{5}{10}$			$\frac{8}{10}$		1

c

		$\frac{3}{10}$	$\frac{4}{10}$		$\frac{6}{10}$			$\frac{9}{10}$	1

d

$\frac{1}{10}$				$\frac{5}{10}$		$\frac{7}{10}$			1

Name: _____ Date: _____

Measuring cylinders

Know how many millilitres are equal to $\frac{1}{4}$, $\frac{1}{2}$, $\frac{3}{4}$ and $\frac{1}{10}$ of 1 litre

Each measuring cylinder can hold 1000 ml or 1 litre.

1 Rule a line across each cylinder to show how full or empty it is when the water reaches the level shown by the label.

2 Colour the amount of water in each cylinder.

You will need:
- ruler
- coloured pencil

A

ml
1000
900
800
700
600
500
400
300
200
100

$\frac{1}{2}$ full

B

ml
1000
900
800
700
600
500
400
300
200
100

$\frac{1}{4}$ full

C

ml
1000
900
800
700
600
500
400
300
200
100

$\frac{2}{10}$ full

D

ml
1000
900
800
700
600
500
400
300
200
100

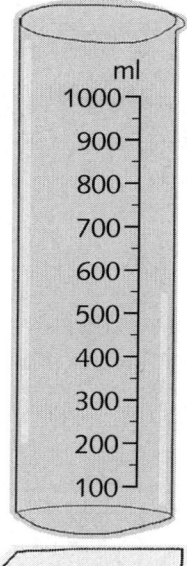

$\frac{1}{4}$ empty

E

ml
1000
900
800
700
600
500
400
300
200
100

$\frac{3}{4}$ empty

F

ml
1000
900
800
700
600
500
400
300
200
100

$\frac{2}{10}$ empty

Name: _____ Date: _____

Fractions full or empty

Know how many millilitres are equal to $\frac{1}{4}$, $\frac{1}{2}$, $\frac{3}{4}$ and $\frac{1}{10}$ of 1 litre

Each cylinder will hold 1000 ml or 1 litre when full.

Complete the labels to show how full or empty each cylinder is when the water reaches the level shown by the label.

a

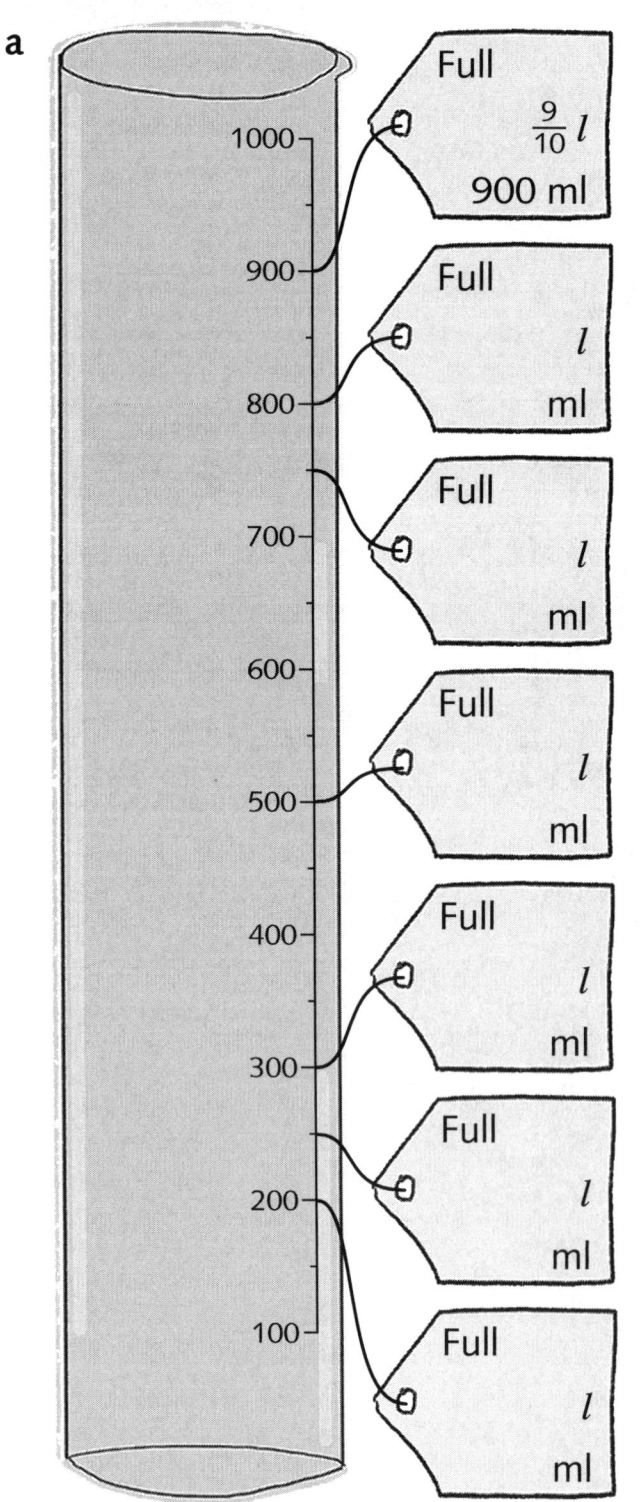

| Full | $\frac{9}{10}$ l |
| 900 ml |

Full | l | ml

Full | l | ml

Full | l | ml

Full | l | ml

Full | l | ml

Full | l | ml

b

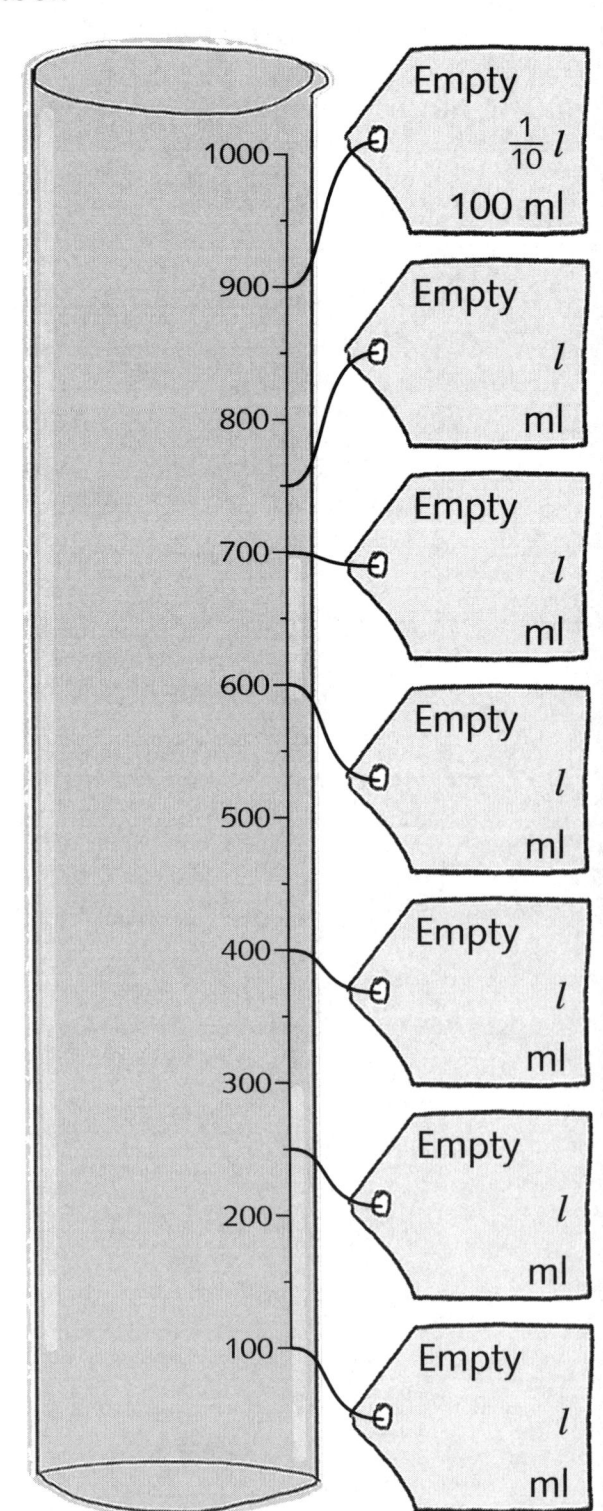

| Empty | $\frac{1}{10}$ l |
| 100 ml |

Empty | l | ml

Empty | l | ml

Empty | l | ml

Empty | l | ml

Empty | l | ml

Empty | l | ml

Name: _____ Date: _____

Go-kart millilitres

Read scales to the nearest 100 millilitres

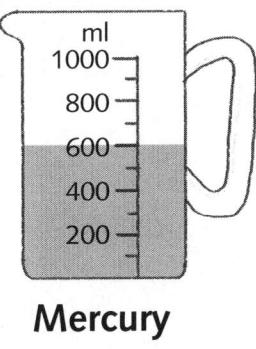
Mercury

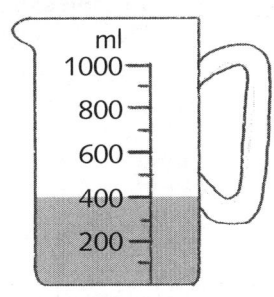
Jupiter

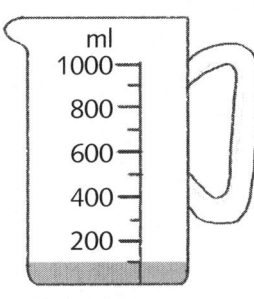
Mars

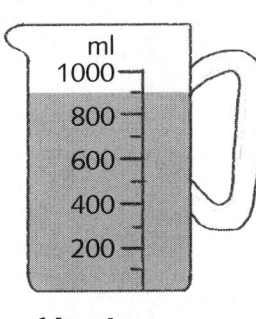
Neptune

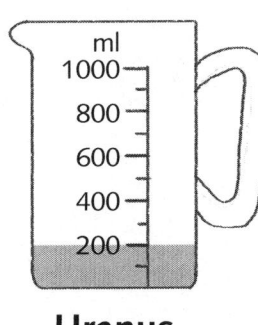
Uranus

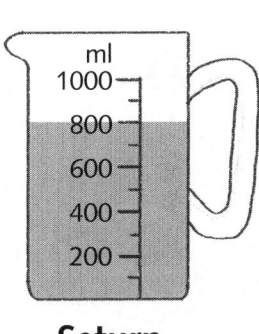
Saturn

1 The jugs above show how much fuel is needed to fill six go-kart engines. Complete the table below.

Go-kart	Fuel in ml	Fuel in litres
Mercury	600 ml	$\frac{6}{10}\,l$
Jupiter		
Mars		
Neptune		
Uranus		
Saturn		
Asteroid		

2 Go-kart Asteroid has 100 ml more fuel than go-kart Jupiter.

Complete the table for Asteroid.

Name: _____ Date: _____

Measuring in millilitres

Measure and compare capacity; use simple scaling
of quantities and equivalents of mixed units

1 On Monday Carlo the ice cream maker measured out these fruit juices.

Write the number of millilitres of juice in each jug.

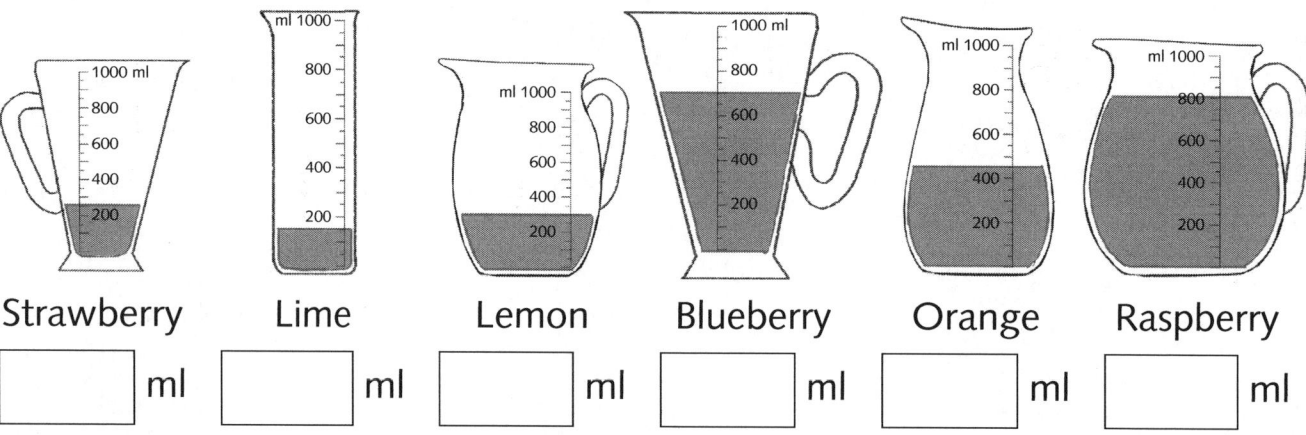

| Strawberry | Lime | Lemon | Blueberry | Orange | Raspberry |

[ ] ml   [ ] ml   [ ] ml   [ ] ml   [ ] ml   [ ] ml

2 To get ready for a busy weekend, on Thursday Carlo measured these
amounts of juice.

Complete the table.

Measurement	Amount of juice	
	in ml	in *l* and ml
a 4 times as much strawberry as on Monday		
b 5 times as much lemon as on Monday		
c 3 times as much raspberry as on Monday		
d 10 times as much lime as on Monday		
e 5 times as much blueberry as on Monday		
f 4 times as much orange as on Monday		

3 How many more millilitres of raspberry juice did he make on Thursday than:

a of orange? [ ]   **b** of lemon? [ ]

Name: _____ Date: _____

stimating

- Add 3-digit numbers using the formal written method of column addition
- Estimate and check the answer to a calculation

1 Rounding numbers to the nearest multiple of 10 helps us to estimate.

a Write the multiples of 10 that the numbers in the middle column come between.

b Circle the one each number is closest to.

Multiple of 10 before		Multiple of 10 after
60	67	⑩
	84	
	172	
	269	
	346	
	378	

2 Estimate the answers to these calculations, then work them out.

Example

354 + 265

Estimate [600]

```
  H  T  O
   3  5  4
+  2  6  5
   6  1  9
   1
```

a 214 + 352

Estimate [ ]

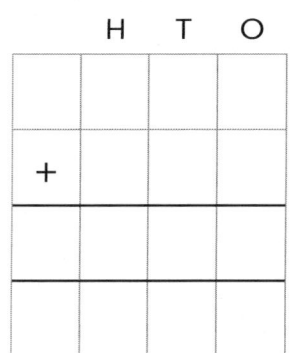

b 289 + 172

Estimate [ ]

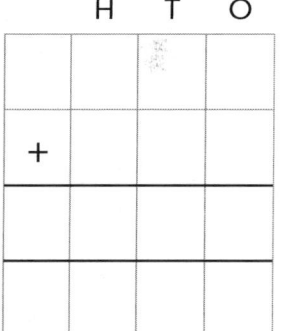

c 341 + 153

Estimate [ ]

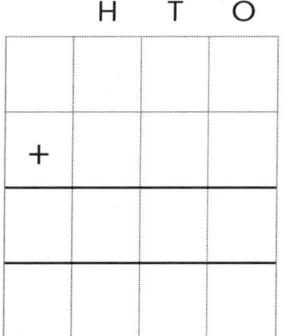

d 346 + 203

Estimate [ ]

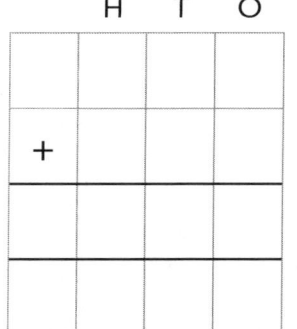

e 378 + 346

Estimate [ ]

Name: _____ Date: _____

Make 900

Add 3-digit numbers using the formal
written method of column addition

1 Roll the dice and fill in the 100s, 10s and 1s digits in the calculations below.

Think about how to make your target number of **900**.

When the digits are filled in, work out the calculation.

Are you near your target?

a 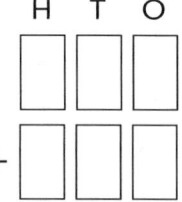   b    c 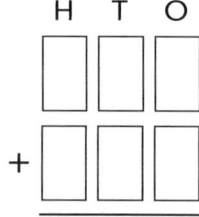   d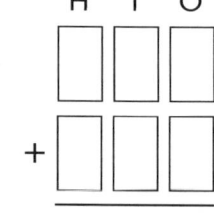

e 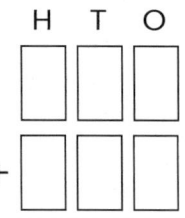   f 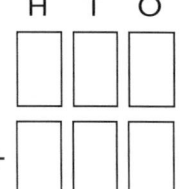   g 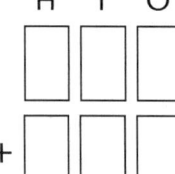   h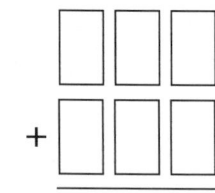

i 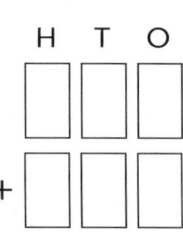   j 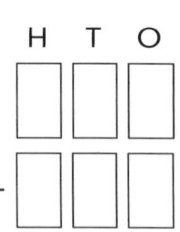   k 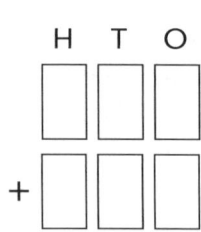   l

2 Which calculation is nearest to 900? How did you decide where to put the digits?

_____

_____

Name: _____ Date: _____

chool shopping

Solve problems involving money and reason mathematically

1 Henry buys a bookcase and pays with £100. How much change will he get?

Calculation: [   ]

Working out:

[   ]

2 Harriet bought a bookcase and a carpet. How much did she spend?

Calculation: [   ]

Working out:

[   ]

3 Henry buys a tablet and art equipment. What will the cost be?

Calculation: [   ]

Working out:

[   ]

4 Harriet buys a CD player and a laptop. How much does she need to pay?

Calculation: [   ]

Working out:

[   ]

Name: _____ Date: _____

Kitting out Thomas

Add and subtract amounts of money

1 Thomas has £500 to spend. He wants to spend his money as wisely as possible.

What different choices does he have? How much will each choice cost?

> **Choice 1**
>
>
>

> **Choice 2**
>
>
>

> **Choice 3**
>
>
>

2 What do you think he should choose? Write your explanation on the back of this sheet.

Name: _____ Date: _____

Break it down

- Subtract 3-digit numbers using the formal method of column subtraction
- Estimate and check the answer to a calculation

1 Estimate the answers to these calculations, then work them out using the formal method of column subtraction.

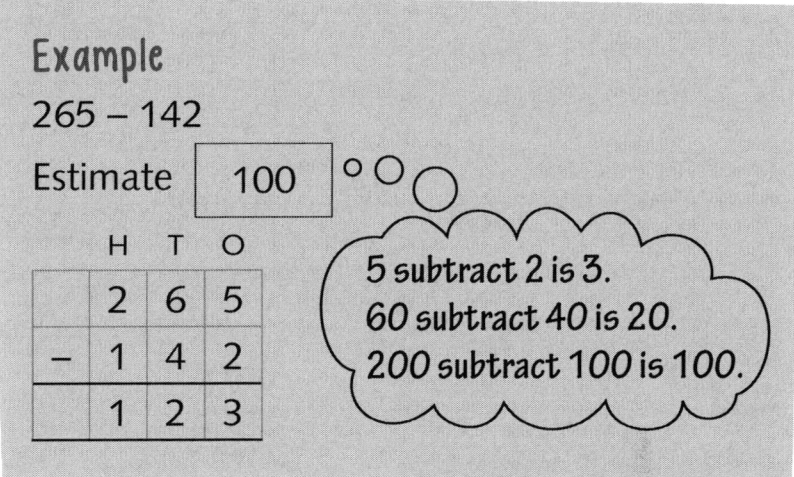

Example

265 – 142

Estimate [100]

	H	T	O
	2	6	5
–	1	4	2
	1	2	3

5 subtract 2 is 3.
60 subtract 40 is 20.
200 subtract 100 is 100.

a 253 – 132

Estimate [   ]

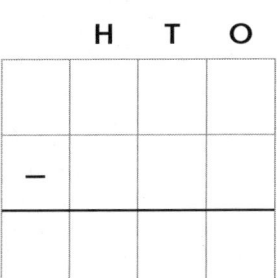

b 286 – 142

Estimate [   ]

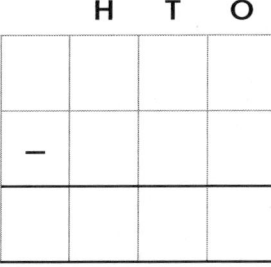

c 379 – 153

Estimate [   ]

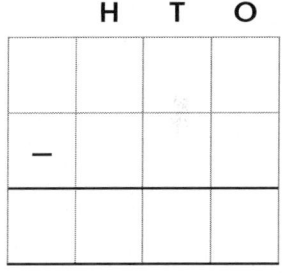

d 384 – 231

Estimate [   ]

e 395 – 173

Estimate [   ]

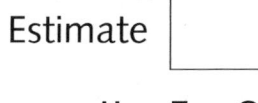

f 478 – 236

Estimate [   ]

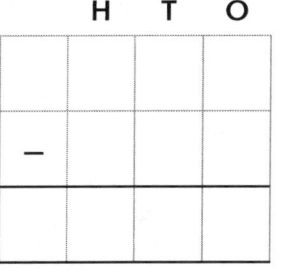

2 Choose four of your calculations and on the back of this sheet check your answers using the inverse operation of addition.

Name: _____ Date: _____

Make 600

Subtract 3-digit numbers using the formal
written method of column subtraction

1 Roll the dice and fill in the 100s, 10s and 1s digits in the calculations below.
Make sure the top number is the larger of the two numbers.

Think about how to make your target number of **600**.

When the digits are filled in, work out the calculation.

Are you near your target?

a H T O 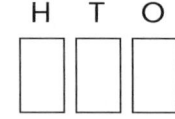 **b** H T O **c** H T O **d** H T O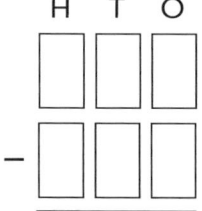

e H T O 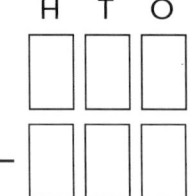 **f** H T O 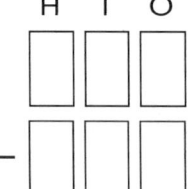 **g** H T O 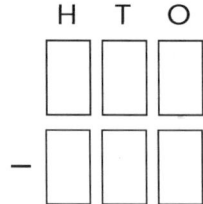 **h** H T O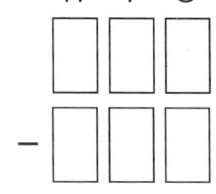

i H T O 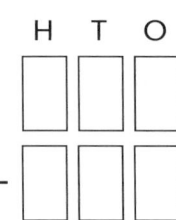 **j** H T O 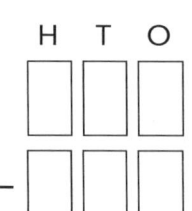 **k** H T O 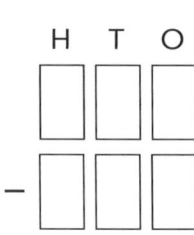 **l** H T O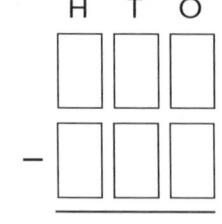

2 Which calculation is nearest to 600?
How did you decide where to put the digits?

_____

_____

Name: _____ Date: _____

Clever jumping

Add numbers mentally

Can you jump from the start number to the target number in the number of jumps stated? You can have two tries at each one!

1 a 448 → 615 in 5 jumps or fewer

448
Start

615
Target

448

615

b 507 → 695 in 5 jumps or fewer

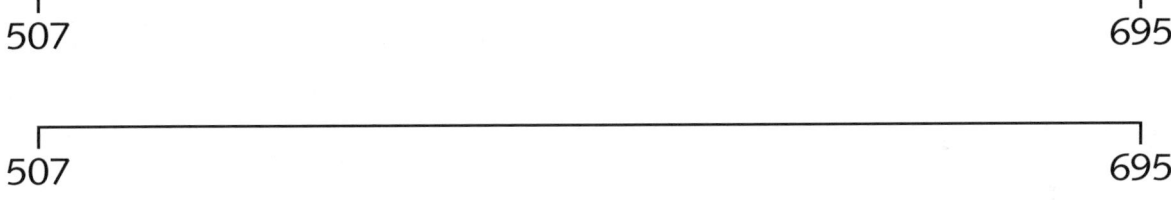

507

695

507

695

c 532 → 748 in 4 jumps or fewer

532

748

532

748

d 567 → 788 in 4 jumps or fewer

567

788

567

788

2 Make up some start and target numbers for a partner.

Name: _____ Date: _____

Jumping backwards

Subtract numbers mentally

Jump back along the number lines from the start number to the target number.

First jump back in jumps of 10 and then 1s.

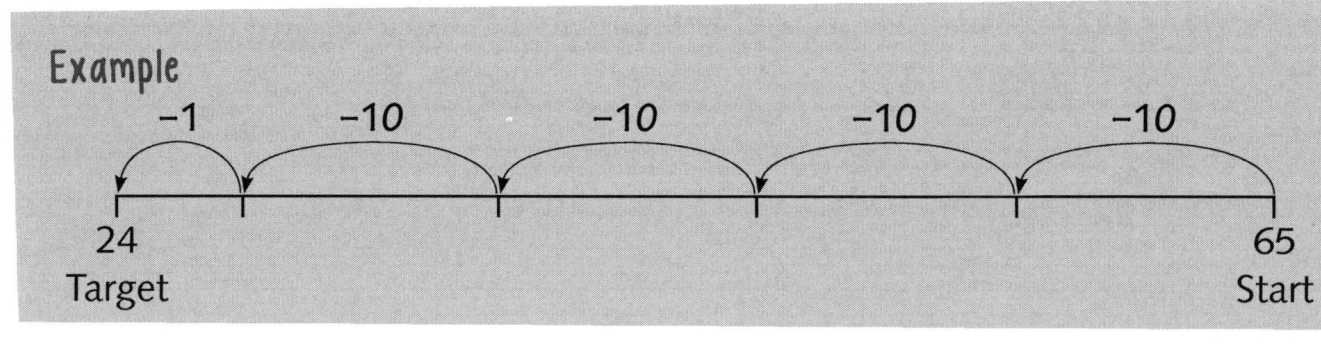

Example

−1   −10   −10   −10   −10

24   65
Target   Start

1

37   74
Target   Start

2

48   89
Target   Start

3

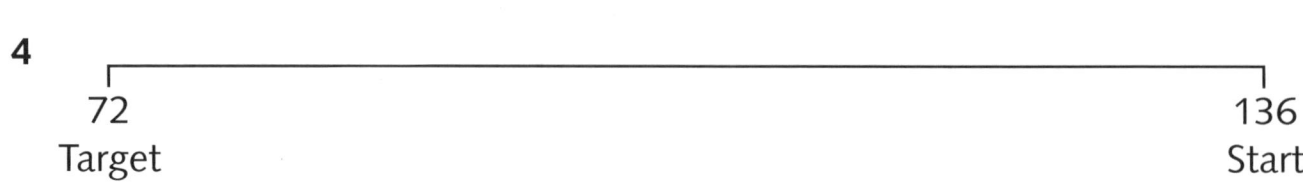

54   104
Target   Start

4

72   136
Target   Start

5

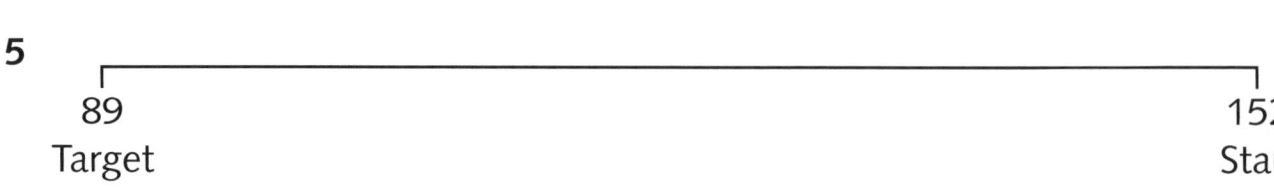

89   152
Target   Start

Name: _____ Date: _____

Digital and wall clocks

Write the time to the minute on 12-hour analogue and digital clocks

Write the missing times on the digital clock and draw the missing hands on the clock face.

1
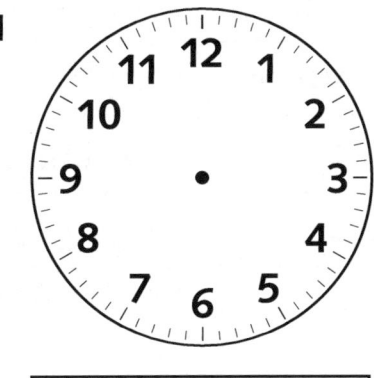

7:35

2

4:16

3

:

4
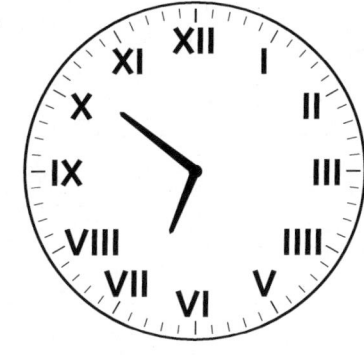

:

5
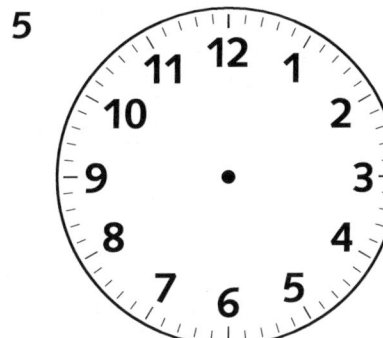

9:47

6
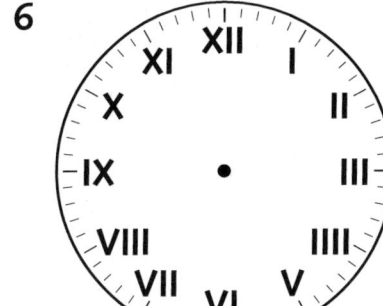

11:32

7

:

8

12:21

9

:

Name: _____ Date: _____

Days of the month

Know the number of days in each month and year

1 Complete the rhyme.

30 days has _____

_____, _____ and _____.

All the rest have 31

except _____ alone

which has _____ days

and _____ days in each leap year

January	July
February	August
March	September
April	October
May	November
June	December

2 Look at the calendar for December.

How many days in December are:

a Fridays?

b Mondays?

c Sundays?

d Wednesdays?

DECEMBER						
M	T	W	Th	F	S	S
	1	2	3	4	5	6
7	8	9	10	11	12	13
14	15	16	17	18	19	20
21	22	23	24	25	26	27
28	29	30	31			

3 Write the day of the week for:

a the first day in December _____

b the last day in December _____

c the first day in January _____

d Christmas Day _____

Name: _____ Date: _____

alendar counting

Know the number of days in each month and year

1 On which days is the Museum:

a always open?

_____

_____

_____

_____

b never open?

_____

c For how many months is it open:

i on a Saturday? ☐ **ii** on a Tuesday? ☐

> ## Fontana Museum
>
> ### Summer Openings
> April – September
> Daily
> Except Sundays
>
> ### Winter Openings
> October – March
> Mon to Thurs only

2 Your class plans to visit the Museum in November.

Cross out the dates in the calendar when:

a the Museum is closed

b your school is closed.

3 Your school visit is in the 3rd week in November. Write the possible dates for the visit.

NOVEMBER						
S	M	T	W	Th	F	S
	1	2	3	4	5	6
7	8	9	10	11	12	13
14	15	16	17	18	19	20
21	22	23	24	25	26	27
28	29	30				

_____

4 Circle the dates when the Museum is open.

18th November   27th November   15th November

21st November   30th November

3rd November   19th November   22nd November

Name: _____ Date: _____

Measuring time

Find the time taken to complete a task or event

Work in a group of about 3 or 4.

Complete this chart to record your times at each station.

Station	Estimated time	Measured time
1		
2		
3		

STATION 1

Estimate then measure the time it will take you to read aloud a verse from a poem.

You will need:
- copy of a verse from a poem
- stopwatch or timer

STATION 2

Estimate then measure how many seconds it will take you to build two tetrahedrons with interlocking tiles.

You will need:
- interlocking equilateral triangles
- stopwatch or seconds timer

STATION 3

Choose a length of time between 20 and 30 seconds.

21...
22...
23...

You will need:
- stopwatch or seconds timer

On your turn and without looking at the stopwatch, stop it when you estimate that you have reached your chosen length of time.

Name: _____ Date: _____

Multiplication using the expanded written method

Use the expanded written method to calculate TO × O

Estimate the answer first then use the expanded written method to work out the answer to these calculations.

Example

$63 \times 8 \rightarrow$ ($60 \times 8 = 480$)

H	T	O	
	6	3	
×		8	
	2	4	(3 × 8)
4	8	0	(60 × 8)
5	0	4	
	1		

1 $45 \times 3 \rightarrow$

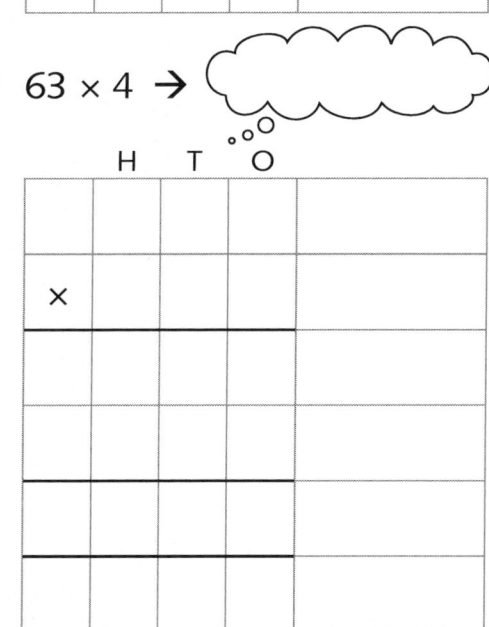

2 $39 \times 5 \rightarrow$

3 $63 \times 4 \rightarrow$

4 $57 \times 4 \rightarrow$

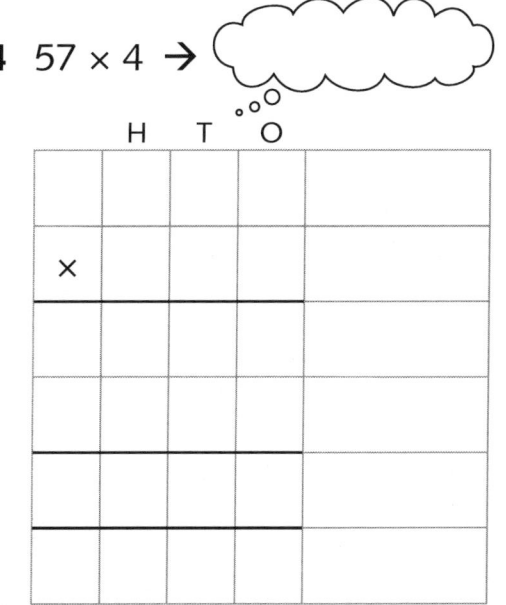

Name: _____ Date: _____

Multiplication: Introducing the formal written method

Use the formal written method to calculate TO × O

Estimate the answer first then use the formal written method to work out the answer to these calculations.

Example

$65 \times 3 \rightarrow$ $70 \times 3 = 210$

	H	T	O
		6	5
×		1	3
	1	9	5

1 $45 \times 3 \rightarrow$

2 $48 \times 5 \rightarrow$

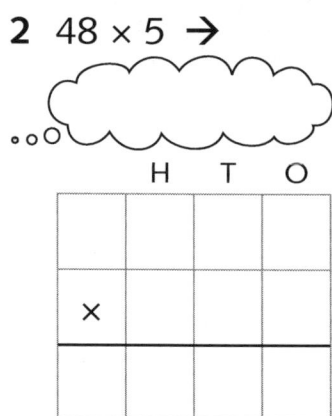

3 $74 \times 3 \rightarrow$

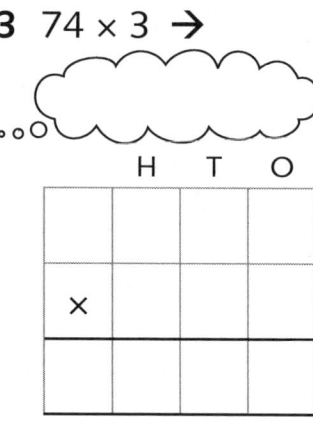

4 $59 \times 4 \rightarrow$

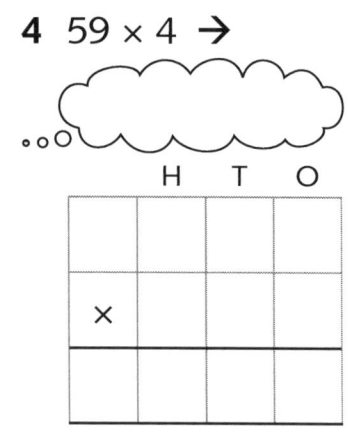

5 $68 \times 3 \rightarrow$

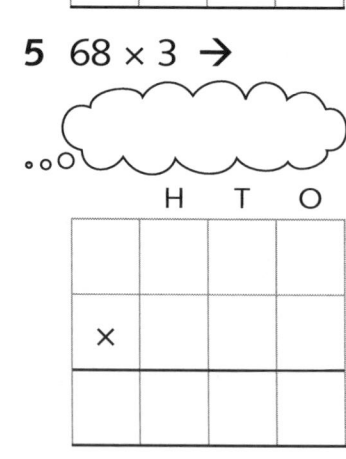

6 $73 \times 4 \rightarrow$

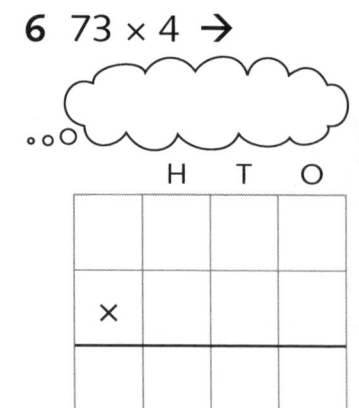

7 $47 \times 4 \rightarrow$

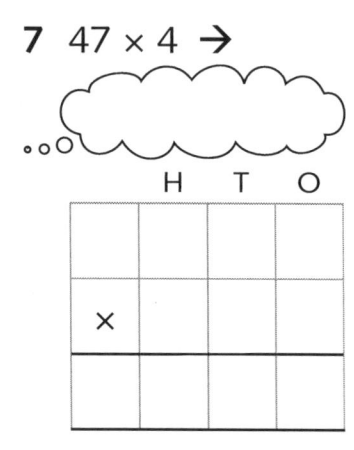

8 $67 \times 5 \rightarrow$

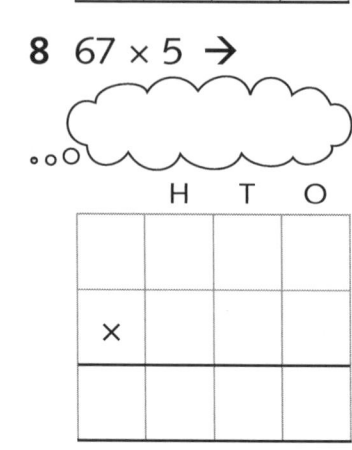

9 $54 \times 8 \rightarrow$

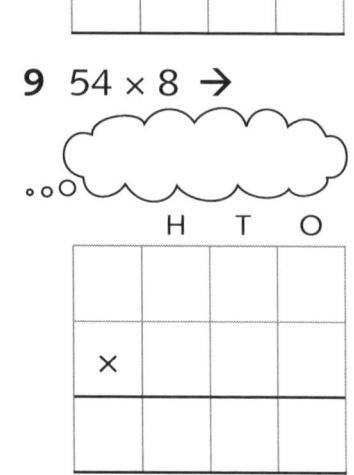

Name: _____ Date: _____

Multiplication: Introducing the formal written method

Use the formal written method to calculate TO × O

1 Estimate the answer first then use the formal written method to work out the answer to these calculations.

Example

68 × 3 → 70 × 3 = 210

	H	T	O
		6	8
×		₂	3
	2	0	4

a 87 × 4 →

	H	T	O
×			

b 76 × 8 →

	H	T	O
×			

c 64 × 3 →

	H	T	O
×			

d 93 × 8 →

	H	T	O
×			

e 79 × 5 →

	H	T	O
×			

f 68 × 8 →

	H	T	O
×			

2 Find the missing numbers in these calculations.

a

	H	T	O
		7	8
×			★
	2	3	4

b

	H	T	O
		6	★
×			8
	5	2	8

c

	H	T	O
		4	8
×			8
	★	★	4

Name: _____ Date: _____

Solving problems

Solve problems and reason mathematically

You will need:
- paper clip and pencil
  – for the spinner
- 16 counters

Play this game with a partner.

- Cover each item on the board with a counter.

- Take turns to:
  - remove a counter from the board
  - spin the spinner
  - multiply the cost of the item by the spinner number (use the method that is best for you)
  - say the answer to the calculation.

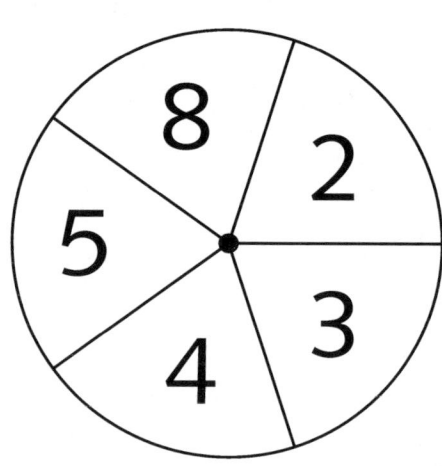

- If you are correct, keep the counter. If you are incorrect, place the counter back on the board.

- Continue until all the counters have been removed.

- The player with the most counters at the end is the winner.

Football £34	Construction set £18	Tennis ball set of 3 £4	Football boots £47
Board game £17	Play kitchen £56	Teddy bear £26	Small bike £79
Wooden building blocks set £25	Toy car £6	Outdoor slippery slide £67	Music player £85
Jigsaw £12	Tennis racquet £38	Doll £19	Hockey stick £27

Name: _____ Date: _____

Division using partitioning

Use partitioning to calculate TO ÷ O

You will need:
• coloured pencils

1 Find and colour the multiples of 3, 2 and 4.

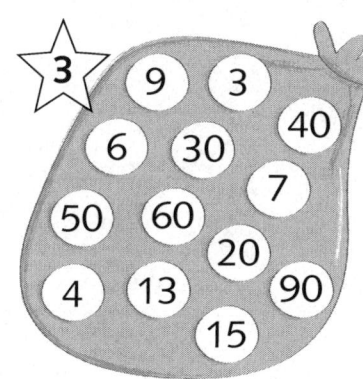

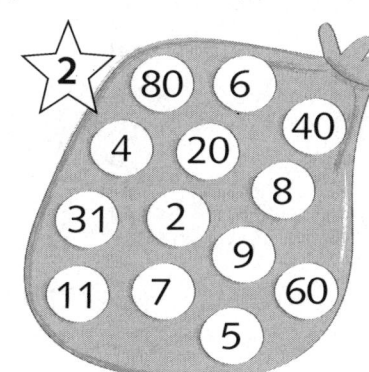

2 Partition each of these numbers to help you find the answer to the division calculation.

a 84 ÷ 3 = [ ]

= [ ]

= [ ]

Example

$69 ÷ 3 = (60 + 9) ÷ 3$
$= 20 + 3$
$= 23$

b 84 ÷ 4 = [ ]

= [ ]

= [ ]

c 93 ÷ 3 = [ ]

= [ ]

= [ ]

d 48 ÷ 4 = [ ]

= [ ]

= [ ]

e 64 ÷ 2 = [ ]

= [ ]

= [ ]

f 66 ÷ 3 = [ ]

= [ ]

= [ ]

g 88 ÷ 4 = [ ]

= [ ]

= [ ]

Name: _____ Date: _____

Division using the formal written method

Use the formal written method to calculate TO ÷ O

Estimate the answer first then use the formal written method to work out the answer to these calculations. Check your answer using the inverse operation.

Example

Estimate: 72 ÷ 3 → (60 ÷ 3 = 20)

	T	O
	2	4
3	7	¹2

		T	O
		2	4
×	₁		3
		7	2

1 75 ÷ 5 →

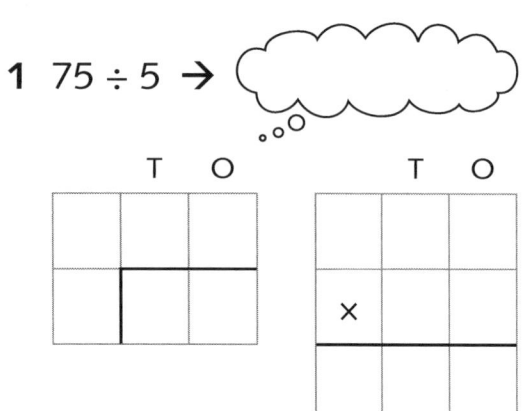

2 64 ÷ 4 →

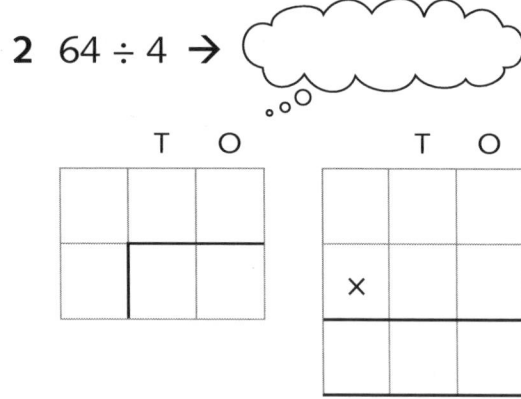

3 56 ÷ 2 →

4 45 ÷ 3 →

5 56 ÷ 4 →

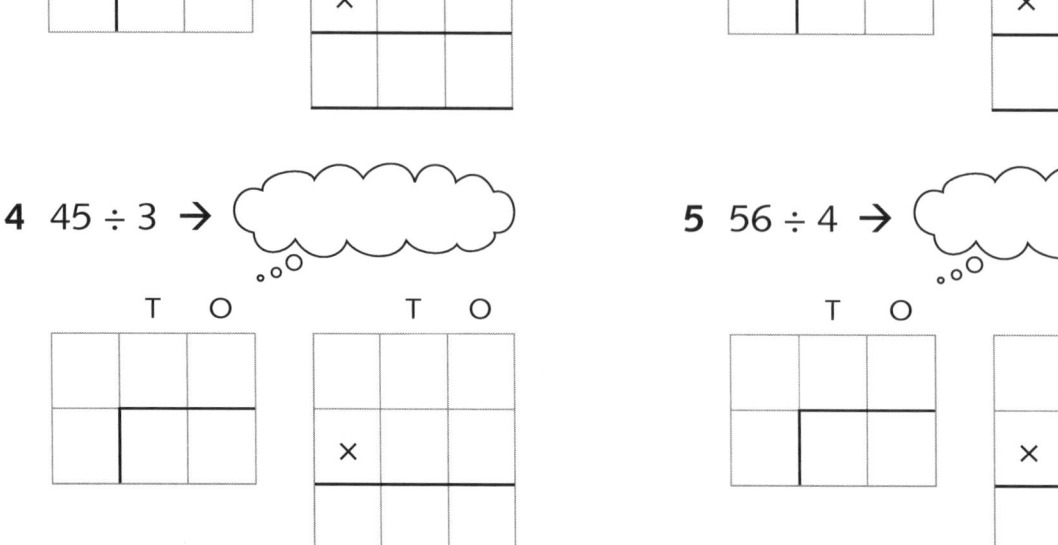

Name: _____ Date: _____

Division using the formal written method

Use the formal written method to calculate TO ÷ O

1 Some of these calculations are not correct. Find the incorrect ones and write the correct calculation and answer.

Example

	T	O
	2	1
3	6	3

a

	T	O
	1	6
4	9	¹2

	T	O

b

	T	O
	2	4
3	8	¹1

	T	O

c

	T	O
	2	4
4	7	¹2

	T	O

d

	T	O
	1	4
8	9	¹6

	T	O

e

	T	O
	1	5
5	7	²5

	T	O

2 Write eight calculations that equal 18. Write two of each operation: addition, subtraction, multiplication and division.

3 Write eight calculations that equal 32. Write two of each operation: addition, subtraction, multiplication and division.

Name: _____ Date: _____

Solving word problems

Solve word problems and reason mathematically

Use the information in the pictures to help solve the problems.

| 64 broccoli | 81 onions | 57 red peppers | 52 sweet corn | 96 carrots |

1 A box of peppers is split into bags of 3. How many bags of red peppers altogether?

2 A chef cuts each sweet corn into 4 pieces. How many pieces can be made from 1 box?

3 Each piece of broccoli is made up of 8 florets. How many florets in one box of broccoli?

4 A box of carrots is split into bags of 4 and a box of onions into bags of 3. Will there be more bags of carrots or onions to sell?

5 To make kebabs for the barbecue, one box of onions, one box of red peppers and one box of sweet corn are used. How many vegetables is this altogether?

6 To make a batch of soup, a chef needs a quarter of a box of broccoli, a third of a box of onions and an eighth of a box of carrots. How many of each vegetable does the chef need?

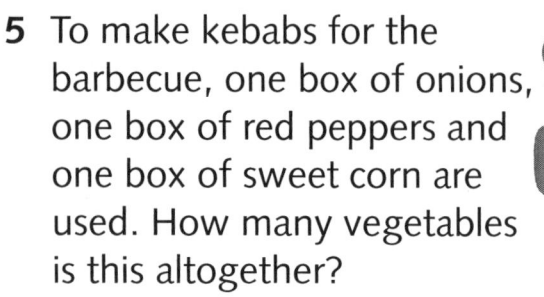

Name: _____ Date: _____

avings bar chart

Show data in a bar chart with intervals labelled in 5s or 10s

You will need:
• coloured pencil

1 Alan puts his savings into these four money banks.

Complete the bar graph to show his savings.

Books 60p   **Games 70p**   **Treats 90p**   **Savings £1**

2 Which money bank has:

a the most money?

_____

b the least money?

_____

c 30p more than
the Books bank?

_____

d 20p less than the
Treats bank?

_____

3 Alan earned this money
for helping his uncle.

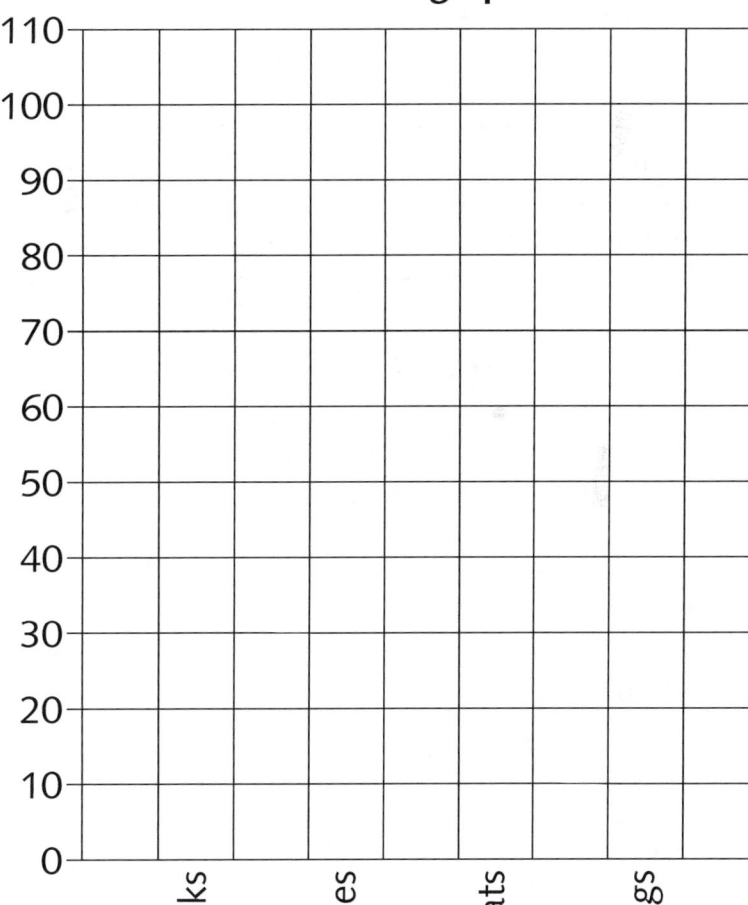

He put the same amount of money into each of his money banks.

Write how much money is now in each bank.

Books [   ]   Games [   ]   Treats [   ]   Savings [   ]

Name: _____ Date: _____

Racing game bar chart

Show data in a bar chart with intervals labelled in 5s or 10s

1 Spin the spinner below.

Record the score on the table in Question 2.

Stop when one score reaches 70.

You will need:
- paper clip and pencil – for the spinner

2 Calculate the total score for each cyclist.

Cyclist	Score	Total
Brad		
Chris		
Jessica		
Laura		

Cycle race results

(Bar chart with Score axis labelled 0, 10, 20, 30, 40, 50, 60, 70 and Cyclist axis labelled Brad, Chris, Jessica, Laura)

3 Complete the bar chart for your scores.

4 a Which cyclist got the highest score?

_____

b What is the difference between the highest and lowest scores?

[ ]

c Write two different statements about the information in your bar chart.

i _____

_____

ii _____

_____

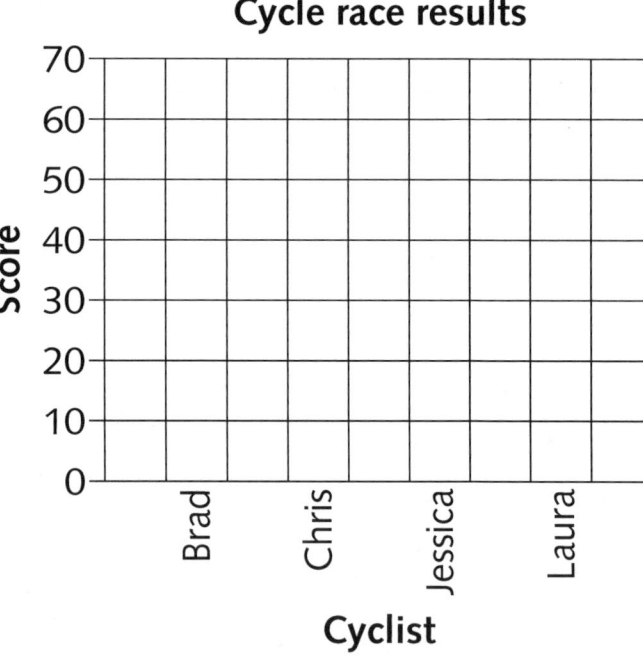

(Spinner: Chris 10 points, Jessica 5 points, Laura 10 points, Brad 5 points)

Name: _____ Date: _____

Dice spots pictogram

Answer questions about data in scaled pictograms and tables

1 a Count the spots on each dice face.

  b Make a tally mark on the table for each number of spots.

  c Count the tally marks and write the total.

Spots	Tally	Total
2		
3		
4		
5		
6		

2 Use the above data to complete the pictogram.

Number of dice

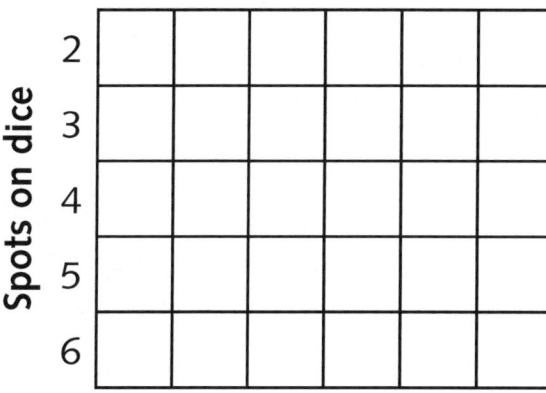

Spots on dice: 2, 3, 4, 5, 6

Key:

■ = 2 dice

◤ = 1 dice

3 a What is the least common number of spots? ☐

  b Which is the more common: 4 spots or 5 spots? ☐

4 How many dice have:

  a more than 4 spots? ☐   **b** fewer than 4 spots? ☐

Name: _____ Date: _____

Bags of fruit bar chart

Answer questions about data in scaled pictograms and tables

The bar chart shows how much fruit is in each bag.

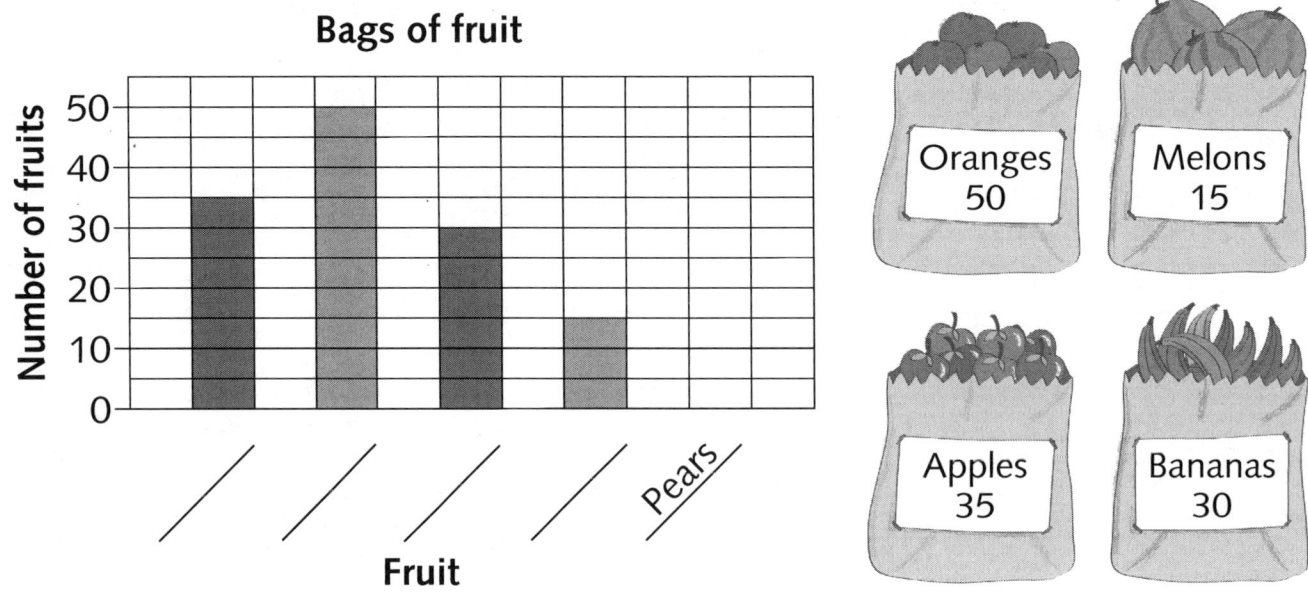

Bags of fruit

Number of fruits

50
40
30
20
10
0

Fruit

Pears

Oranges 50

Melons 15

Apples 35

Bananas 30

1 Write the name of each fruit on the horizontal axis.

2 Which bag has:

   a the most fruit? _____   **b** the least fruit? _____

3 How many more apples are there than:

   a bananas? [ ]   **b** melons? [ ]

4 Draw a bar in the chart to show the number of pears in the bag.

Pears 40

5 How many fewer pears are there than oranges? [ ]

6 A chef makes a bowl of fruit salad.

   He uses 5 apples, 2 oranges, 4 bananas, 1 melon and 3 pears.

   How much of each fruit is left?

   apples [ ]   oranges [ ]   bananas [ ]

   melons [ ]   pears [ ]